Endorsements for the Flourish Bible Study Series

"The brilliant and beautiful mix of sound teaching, helpful charts, lists, sidebars, and appealing graphics—as well as insightful questions that get the reader into the text of Scripture—make these studies that women will want to invest time in and will look back on as time well spent."

Nancy Guthrie, Bible teacher; author, *Even Better than Eden*

"My daughter and I love using Flourish Bible Studies for our morning devotions. Lydia Brownback's faithful probing of biblical texts; insightful questions; invitations to engage in personal applications using additional biblical texts and historical contexts; and commitment to upholding the whole counsel of God as it bears on living life as a godly woman have drawn us closer to the Lord and to his word. Brownback never sidesteps hard questions or hard providences, but neither does she appeal to discourses of victimhood or therapy, which are painfully common in the genre of women's Bible studies. I cannot recommend this series highly enough. My daughter and I look forward to working through this whole series together!"

Rosaria Butterfield, Former Professor of English, Syracuse University; author, *The Gospel Comes with a House Key*

"As a women's ministry leader, I am excited about the development of the Flourish Bible Study series, which will not only prayerfully equip women to increase in biblical literacy but also come alongside them to build a systematic and comprehensive framework to become lifelong students of the word of God. This series provides visually engaging studies with accessible content that will not only strengthen the believer but the church as well."

Karen Hodge, Coordinator of Women's Ministries, Presbyterian Church in America; coauthor, *Transformed*

"Lydia Brownback is an experienced Bible teacher who has dedicated her life to ministry roles that help women (and men) grow in Christ. With a wealth of biblical, historical, and theological content, her Flourish Bible Studies are ideal for groups and individuals that are serious about the in-depth study of the word of God."

Phil and Lisa Ryken, President, Wheaton College; and his wife, Lisa

"If you're looking for rich, accessible, and deeply biblical Bible studies, this series is for you! Lydia Brownback leads her readers through different books of the Bible, providing background information, maps, timelines, and questions that probe the text in order to glean understanding and application. She settles us deeply in the context of a book as she highlights God's unfolding plan of redemption and rescue. You will learn, you will delight in God's word, and you will love our good King Jesus even more."

Courtney Doctor, Coordinator of Women's Initiatives, The Gospel Coalition; author, *From Garden to Glory* and *Steadfast*

"Lydia Brownback's Bible study series provides a faithful guide to book after book. You'll find rich insights into context and good questions to help you study and interpret the Bible. Page by page, the studies point you to respond to each passage and to love our great and gracious God. I will recommend the Flourish series for years to come for those looking for a wise, Christ-centered study that leads toward the goal of being transformed by the word."

Taylor Turkington, Bible teacher; Director, BibleEquipping.org

"Lydia Brownback has a contagious love for the Bible. Not only is she fluent in the best of biblical scholarship in the last generation, but her writing is accessible to the simplest of readers. She has the rare ability of being clear without being reductionistic. I anticipate many women indeed will flourish through her trustworthy guidance in this series."

David Mathis, Senior Teacher and Executive Editor, desiringGod.org; Pastor, Cities Church, Saint Paul, Minnesota; author, *Habits of Grace*

"Lydia Brownback's Flourish Bible Study series has been a huge gift to the women's ministry in my local church. Many of our groups have gone through her studies in both the Old and New Testaments and have benefited greatly. The Flourish Bible Study series is now my go-to for a combination of rich Bible study, meaningful personal application, and practical group interaction. I recommend them whenever a partner in ministry asks me for quality women's Bible study resources. I'm so thankful Brownback continues to write them and share them with us!"

Jen Oshman, author, *Enough about Me* and *Cultural Counterfeits*; Women's Ministry Director, Redemption Parker, Colorado

ECCLESIASTES

Flourish Bible Study Series
By Lydia Brownback

FLOURISH
BIBLE STUDY

ECCLESIASTES

FINDING MEANING WHEN LIFE FEELS MEANINGLESS

LYDIA BROWNBACK

WHEATON, ILLINOIS

Ecclesiastes: Finding Meaning When Life Feels Meaningless

© 2024 by Lydia Brownback

Published by Crossway
    1300 Crescent Street
    Wheaton, Illinois 60187

Cover design: Crystal Courtney

First printing 2024

Printed in China

Trade paperback ISBN: 978-1-4335-8328-5

Crossway is a publishing ministry of Good News Publishers.

RRDS   33 32 31 30 29 28 27 26 25 24
15 14 13 12 11 10 9 8 7 6 5 4 3 2 1

With gratitude to God
for Russ

With all my heart, I hope you'll hear the Preacher's message.

"For everything there is a season, and a time for every matter under heaven.
. . . He has made everything beautiful in its time." —Ecclesiastes 3:1, 11

CONTENTS

THE PLACE OF ECCLESIASTES
IN BIBLICAL HISTORY

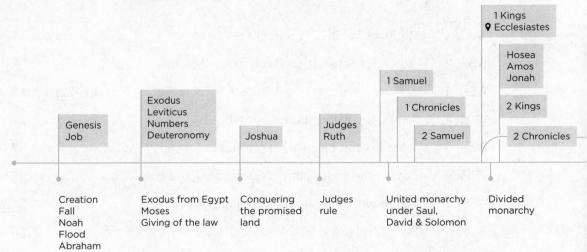

1 Kings
📍 Ecclesiastes

Hosea
Amos
Jonah

1 Samuel

1 Chronicles

2 Kings

Exodus
Leviticus
Numbers
Deuteronomy

Genesis
Job

Joshua

Judges
Ruth

2 Samuel

2 Chronicles

Creation
Fall
Noah
Flood
Abraham

Exodus from Egypt
Moses
Giving of the law

Conquering
the promised
land

Judges
rule

United monarchy
under Saul,
David & Solomon

Divided
monarchy

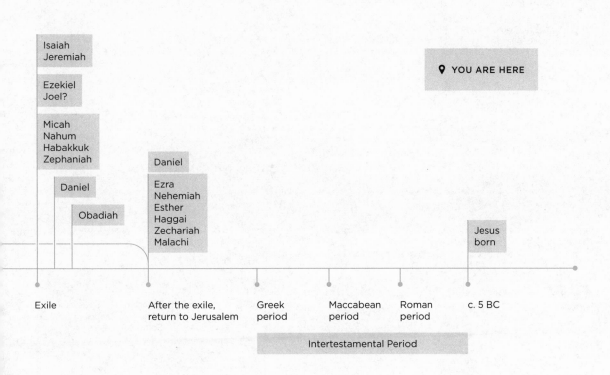

INTRODUCTION

GETTING INTO ECCLESIASTES

Happiness is right around the corner—or is it? We don't say it out loud, and we might not consciously think it, but somewhere in the stresses of the right here, right now of our lives, we suspect it's true. Maybe the new job, that other church, or a different set of friends will finally bring about the satisfaction and meaning we can't seem to hold on to. As we live in the rhythms of our routine lives, we can't help but wonder, in our quieter moments, if there's meaning in all this mundane. What's the point of it all?

That's exactly what the Preacher, the author of Ecclesiastes, determined to find out. He embarked on a quest for meaning and purpose, using his acquired wisdom as his guide. Over the next ten weeks we will follow him on his "purpose journey" as he recounts what he saw and experienced and ultimately discovered. His journey wasn't easy, so get ready for some heavy stuff. This is no lighthearted Bible book! But we'll find joy mixed in. And hope. We'll also learn about true, biblical wisdom and how to live wisely in whatever circumstances God has placed us. Most of all, we'll be guided toward our Savior, the Lord Jesus Christ.

WHO'S WHO IN ECCLESIASTES

The Preacher is the primary figure in Ecclesiastes. This title, "Preacher," is an English translation of the Hebrew word *Qohelet*. (The Greek translation of *Qohelet* is *Ekklēsiastēs*, which is how the book gets its title.) The traditional view is that Israel's King Solomon is "the Preacher" who wrote the book as a way of reflecting on his life in his old age and passing along the wisdom he gained. Today, however, many scholars believe someone else wrote it, perhaps borrowing Solomon's name and reputation to lend weight to the message. Our study takes the traditional view, that the author was Solomon himself. After all, the Bible itself points us this way. In the very first verse of Ecclesiastes, the author identifies himself as King David's son and as king in Jerusalem. He also claims to excel in

Key Terms in Ecclesiastes

Fear God: The Bible's Wisdom Books teach that the essence of wisdom is to live in the "fear of the Lᴏʀᴅ" (Proverbs 9:10). This is the conclusion the Preacher reaches here in Ecclesiastes (12:13). It's to love what God loves (righteousness) and hate what he hates (sin).

Folly / Fool: In the Bible's Wisdom Literature, fools are those who reject the Lord God to embrace sin and worldliness, which leads ultimately to ruin.

Striving after wind: Linked with the word *vanity*, the phrase is another way the Preacher conveys futility.

Under the sun: The Preacher uses this expression frequently to refer to life in a fallen world.

Vanity: The original word used by the Preacher was *hebel*, a Hebrew word that we translate as "vanity" or "vain." It means "vapor" or "mist" and is used to indicate something that is elusive or fleeting.

Wind: In the Bible, the word *ruah* is translated as "wind," "breath," or "spirit" depending on context.

Wisdom / Wise: To be wise is to revolve oneself—affections, thoughts, decisions, actions—on God and his kingdom. The result is "skill in the art of godly living."[1]

wisdom more than anyone else (1:16), which ties back to Solomon's story in 1 Kings. There, in answer to Solomon's prayer, the Lord responded:

> "Behold, I give you a wise and discerning mind, so that none like you has been before you and none like you shall arise after you. I give you also what you have not asked, both riches and honor, so that no other king shall compare with you, all your days." (1 Kings 3:12–13)

Solomon went on to become the wealthiest king in world history at that time. Regrettably, Solomon rejected the wisdom he'd been granted, making terrible relationship decisions that led him away from the Lord and also abusing those under his authority. If you read Solomon's history in 1 Kings, it's very easy to see the connection to the Preacher's story in Ecclesiastes. This biblical evidence is why we will approach our study of Ecclesiastes as though Solomon wrote it.

Although the Preacher is the primary figure in Ecclesiastes, he is not the most important. That honor belongs to God, who, even when not explicitly mentioned, underlies and overarches every single aspect of the book. His special covenant name, Yahweh, which appears as Lord in our Bibles (with small capital letters) is not found in Ecclesiastes. Instead the Preacher uses *Elohim*, which we translate as "God," most likely because he shaped his book not only for God's people but also for those outside of Israel who did not yet know Yahweh.[2]

In Ecclesiastes we also find people who are righteous and wise and others who are wicked and foolish. In the Bible's Wisdom Literature, *the wise* are those who orient their entire lives around God and his ways. *Fools* are those who reject God and the paths of righteousness and suffer personal and relational destruction as a result.

SETTING

Bible scholars and pastors over the centuries have been baffled by Ecclesiastes. Some find this book utterly depressing and lacking in any sort of cohesive message. There isn't one agreed-upon opinion of who wrote it, when it was written, and what the takeaways should be. Bible scholars even disagree about when Ecclesiastes was written. If Solomon was indeed the author, we can assume it was written in the latter part of his life (he was Israel's king from about 970–930 BC).

THEMES

Ecclesiastes is one of the Bible's Wisdom Books, which also include Job and Proverbs, and a few of the psalms can be classified as wisdom psalms. The overarching theme of the Wisdom Books is, of course, *wisdom*, but biblical wisdom isn't so much about head knowledge as about heart knowledge. Biblical wisdom is defined as "the fear of the Lord" (Proverbs 9:7), which is all about living by, under, and for God and his ways. Threaded throughout Ecclesiastes are *the effects of sin*, which permeated the world after the fall of Adam and Eve in Genesis 3. The Bible tells us that because of sin, "the whole creation has been groaning" (Romans 8:22), and all this groaning is put on display in Ecclesiastes. The word *vanity* appears numerous times in the book, a word that means "vapor," or "elusive."[3] *Enjoyment* is a surprising theme in this somber book, but it stands out all the more clearly in all this somberness. Finally, the Preacher compels us to think a good bit about *death* as we make our way through the study.

> *"Ecclesiastes was written in order for us to despair in ourselves and depend on our joyous God and his blessed will for our lives."*[4]

STUDYING ECCLESIASTES

Ecclesiastes has both poetry and prose, and it's helpful to know a bit about how to approach these genres as we begin our study. Simply put, poetry is an art form, and therefore we aren't to take each word literally the way we are with narrative prose. More generally, we can keep in mind the unique ways the Preacher writes: "As a genuine wisdom teacher, he has a gift for penetrating observation and for stating things in a profound and challenging manner that spur the listener on to deeper thought and reflection."[5]

At the beginning of each week's lesson, read the entire passage. And then read it again. Marinating in the Scripture text is the most important part of any Bible study.

GROUP STUDY

If you are doing this study as part of a group, you'll want to finish each week's lesson before the group meeting. As you prepare, you can work your way through the study questions all in one sitting or by doing a little bit each day. And don't be discouraged if you don't have sufficient time to answer every question. Just do as much as you can, knowing that the more you do, the more you'll learn. No matter how much of the study you are able to complete each week, the group will benefit simply from your presence, so don't skip the gathering if you can't finish! That being said, group time will be most rewarding for every participant if you have done the lesson in advance. When you gather, read the entire passage aloud before your discussion time. Then you can discuss your answers to the questions, or just talk through the Scripture passage, using your lesson prep to guide your discussion.

If you are leading the group, you can download the free leader's guide at https://www.lydiabrownback.com/flourish-series.

INDIVIDUAL STUDY

The study is designed to run for ten weeks, but you can set your own pace if you're studying solo. And you can download the free leader's guide (https://www.lydiabrownback.com/flourish-series) if you'd like some guidance along the way.

Marinating in the Scripture text is the most important part of any Bible study.

Reading Plan

	Primary Text	Supplemental Reading
Week 1	Ecclesiastes 1:1–18	Genesis 3:17–19; Romans 8:20
Week 2	Ecclesiastes 2:1–26	1 Kings 4:21–34; 11:1–3
Week 3	Ecclesiastes 3:1–22	Psalm 107
Week 4	Ecclesiastes 4:1–16	
Week 5	Ecclesiastes 5:1–6:12	Luke 12:13–21
Week 6	Ecclesiastes 7:1–29	
Week 7	Ecclesiastes 8:1–17	
Week 8	Ecclesiastes 9:1–18	
Week 9	Ecclesiastes 10:1–11:6	
Week 10	Ecclesiastes 11:7–12:14	1 Corinthians 1:18–31

VANITY OF VANITIES!

ECCLESIASTES 1:1-18

Elevator rides are rarely memorable, but one in particular lingers in my mind. On-boarding with me were several men, obviously together as business colleagues, and, in unspoken but universally understood elevator protocol, we began the descent in silence. As we neared ground level, the businessmen tossed out a comment or two about sports and lunch, and then one of them said, "Hey, today's my birthday." Another uncomfortably long silence immediately followed until one of his colleagues took pity on him and replied, "Hey, man, that's great. Hope it's a good one." It was so awkward! There's something off-putting about self-stated birthday announcements, isn't there? They seem so, well, attention-seeking and convey a desire to be celebrated. But a more charitable interpretation results if we realize that most people aren't so much looking to be *celebrated* as simply *remembered*. That very human longing is brought front and center in this week's lesson, and we'll see that it goes much deeper than birthdays.

1. VANITY OF VANITIES (1:1-3)

The author identifies himself in the very first verse:

> ¹The words of the Preacher, the son of David, king in Jerusalem. (v. 1)

He refers to himself as "the Preacher," which is the way our English Bible translates the original Hebrew word *Qohelet*. It can also be rendered "Convener" or "Collector." Since many of King David's descendants rose to kingship and ruled from Jerusalem, we have no way of identifying which one is in view in verse 1, but in the chapters ahead, there are clues that this particular king was likely David's son Solomon. As we noted in the introduction, many scholars believe, for a variety of reasons, that the author was someone else, but the plainest reading of the text points to Solomon. For the purposes of our study, identifying the author isn't what ultimately matters—it's grasping his message.

After his personal introduction, the author announces his overarching theme:

> ² Vanity of vanities, says the Preacher,
>   vanity of vanities! All is vanity. (v. 2)

We find this exact expression, "Vanity of vanities," only twice in the book—here and near the very end (12:8). It's the Preacher's way of bookending his primary point.

✦ Notice how many times in just this one verse that he uses the word *vanity*! The original Hebrew word conveys the idea of vapor or mist, something fleeting or elusive.[6] To what does the Preacher apply this term *vanity* here in verse 2?

_____

_____

_____

_____

The Preacher is going to back up his vanity claim with several examples. He begins with man's work:

> ³ What does man gain by all the toil
>   at which he toils under the sun? (v. 3)

✦ Here Solomon asks what's called a "rhetorical question," which is a question with an obvious answer. In light of the expression he uses in verse 2, what is the answer to his question in verse 3?

_____

_____

_____

_____

2. FROM HERE TO THERE (1:4-7)

The Preacher backs up his thesis, that everything is vanity, with observations from nature:

> ⁴ A generation goes, and a generation comes,
>   but the earth remains forever.
> ⁵ The sun rises, and the sun goes down,
>   and hastens to the place where it rises.
> ⁶ The wind blows to the south
>   and goes around to the north;
> around and around goes the wind,
>   and on its circuits the wind returns.
> ⁷ All streams run to the sea,
>   but the sea is not full;
> to the place where the streams flow,
>   there they flow again. (vv. 4–7)

✦ In what way do these natural occurrences reinforce the Preacher's theme?

....

....

....

....

3. NOTHING NEW (1:8-11)

The Preacher goes on to describe the sameness of life from generation to generation:

> ⁸ All things are full of weariness;
>   a man cannot utter it;
> the eye is not satisfied with seeing,
>   nor the ear filled with hearing.
> ⁹ What has been is what will be,
>   and what has been done is what will be done,
>   and there is nothing new under the sun.
> ¹⁰ Is there a thing of which it is said,
>   "See, this is new"?

It has been already
    in the ages before us.
" There is no remembrance of former things,
    nor will there be any remembrance
of later things yet to be
    among those who come after. (vv. 8–11)

✦ We can summarize his poetic description this way: life on this earth is unsatisfying. What does Psalm 63:1–5 reveal about where all this earthly dissatisfaction is intended to direct us?

✦ Summarize what the Preacher says in Ecclesiastes 1:8–11 about the ultimate end of every earthly endeavor.

✦ There is only one way to alter the outcome of what the Preacher describes in verses 8–11. According to 1 Corinthians 15:58, what is that alternate way?

4. A NOBLE QUEST (1:12-13)

Now the Preacher begins to share his personal experience. Linking the Preacher with Solomon seems logical, based on what he writes here:

> ¹² I the Preacher have been king over Israel in Jerusalem. ¹³ And I applied my heart to seek and to search out by wisdom all that is done under heaven. It is an unhappy business that God has given to the children of man to be busy with. (vv. 12–13)

Not only does the Preacher remind us of his kingship; he also describes how he applied wisdom to understand the way the world works. If we look back at what the Historical Books of the Bible tells us about Solomon, we're told, "God gave Solomon wisdom and understanding beyond measure, and breadth of mind like the sand on the seashore, so that Solomon's wisdom surpassed the wisdom of all the people of the east and all the wisdom of Egypt" (1 Kings 4:29–30). The connection between this history of King Solomon and the words of the Preacher here in Ecclesiastes are by no means definitive, but it certainly gives us a valid reason to link them.

✦ What conclusion does the Preacher reach in verses 12–13 as a result of his search?

....

....

....

....

✦ After Adam and Eve sinned in the garden of Eden, unbroken fellowship with God and the paradise they'd enjoyed in the garden were over. As a result of their sin, life for all mankind would be very different thereafter. What link do you see between God's words to Adam in Genesis 3:17–19 and the words of the Preacher here in Ecclesiastes 1:13?

....

....

....

....

✦ If we are wise like the Preacher, we won't refuse to face the reality he describes—much of life is "an unhappy business" (v. 13). And as we look back on Genesis 3, wisdom calls us to face the reason for this unhappiness—sin. Only as we face this reality will our hearts be gripped by our need for help and hope. How does Romans 8:20–21 provide this help and hope?

5. STRIVING AFTER WIND (1:14–15)

The Preacher continues his recall and concludes twice, each time with a proverb, that everything is "a striving after wind." First is this:

> ¹⁴ I have seen everything that is done under the sun, and behold, all is vanity and a striving after wind.
>
> ¹⁵ What is crooked cannot be made straight,
> and what is lacking cannot be counted. (vv. 14–15)

✦ We can best understand his word "crooked" not as something bent or broken but as something unknowable or hidden. What do you think his proverb in verse 15 means, and how does it reinforce his thesis, that everything is "a striving after wind" (v. 14)?

"People say, 'It is what it is.' On the contrary, it is not what it could have been. We all live east of Eden."[7]

6. SOLOMON'S QUEST (1:16–18)

After setting out his credentials once again, he repeats the pattern:

¹⁶ I said in my heart, "I have acquired great wisdom, surpassing all who were over Jerusalem before me, and my heart has had great experience of wisdom and knowledge." ¹⁷ And I applied my heart to know wisdom and to know madness and folly. I perceived that this also is but a striving after wind.

¹⁸   For in much wisdom is much vexation,
   and he who increases knowledge increases sorrow. (vv. 16–18)

✦ What is his point in verse 18, and what makes it "a striving after wind"?

LET'S TALK

1. Each one of us has a craving to be remembered, to leave a lasting mark on the world. Where do you observe this in your world, and how does this craving show up in your own life?

2. In our information age, we crave knowledge and wisdom. Discuss where and how you've seen the Preacher's proverb—"In much wisdom is much vexation, and he who increases knowledge increases sorrow" (1:18)—play out in your life and in the world around you.

SEARCH FOR SATISFACTION

ECCLESIASTES 2:1-26

Pleasure can't be hoarded, but that doesn't stop us from trying at times. If a slice of chocolate cake is good, two are better, we reason, but after indulging in that second slice we often feel bloated and ashamed of ourselves. Cake pleasure isn't the only lure. As pleasure-seekers, we grab onto possessions, work accolades, personal space, adrenaline highs, and vocal prominence in conversations. The hoarding possibilities are endless, and with each new enjoyment, we can be tricked into believing that since a little is good, more will be better. But it never works. God has hardwired the world in such a way that those who live for pleasure are sure to miss it—or lose it pretty quickly. Simply put, to live for pleasure is to waste our lives. The Preacher discovered this firsthand, and we can put a lot of stock in his evaluation since he had unlimited resources to engage in the "more is better" test. He lays it all out for us this week.

1. A PLEASURE TEST (2:1-3)

Having acquired wisdom (1:16), the Preacher now looks back on his quest to find meaning, purpose, and satisfaction:

> ¹I said in my heart, "Come now, I will test you with pleasure; enjoy yourself." But behold, this also was vanity. ²I said of laughter, "It is mad," and of pleasure, "What use is it?" ³I searched with my heart how to cheer my body with wine—my heart still guiding me with wisdom—and how to lay hold on folly, till I might see what was good for the children of man to do under heaven during the few days of their life. (vv. 1–3)

✦ What sort of pleasures did the Preacher pursue here?

....

....

....

✦ In the course of this test, what kept him from the inevitable destruction of decadent overindulgence?

....

....

....

....

✦ What was the result of his pleasure test?

....

....

....

....

2. LIFE AT THE TOP (2:4-8)

The Preacher, being a great king, had great power, which enabled him to experience things that most people never do:

> ⁴I made great works. I built houses and planted vineyards for myself. ⁵I made myself gardens and parks, and planted in them all kinds of fruit trees. ⁶I made myself pools from which to water the forest of growing trees. ⁷I bought male and female slaves, and had slaves who were born in my house. I had also great possessions of herds and flocks, more than any who had been before me in Jerusalem. ⁸I also gathered for myself silver and gold and the treasure of kings and provinces. I got singers, both men and women, and many concubines, the delight of the sons of man. (vv. 4–8)

✢ Identify from verses 4–8 the power, possessions, and pleasures he experienced:

· Power:

_____

_____

_____

· Possessions:

_____

_____

_____

· Pleasures:

_____

_____

_____

✢ Look back on all the Preacher did in his pursuit of satisfaction. For whom did he do all these things?[8]

_____

_____

_____

_____

> "God's presence and God's presents
> are the reasons to rejoice."[9]

3. NO HOLDS BARRED (2:9–11)

From a worldly standpoint, the Preacher certainly lacked for nothing! And being a realist, he wasn't embarrassed to admit it:

> ⁹ So I became great and surpassed all who were before me in Jerusalem. Also my wisdom remained with me. ¹⁰ And whatever my eyes desired I did not keep from them. I kept my heart from no pleasure, for my heart found pleasure in all my toil, and this was my reward for all my toil. ¹¹ Then I considered all that my hands had done and the toil I had expended in doing it, and behold, all was vanity and a striving after wind, and there was nothing to be gained under the sun. (vv. 9–11)

✦ This God-appointed king of Israel says that he experienced pleasure in his accomplishments, but then, when he really thought about it, there was no real gain. This, too, was "vanity and a striving after wind." What seems glaringly absent from his pursuits, and how might that explain why he was unable to hold onto his delight in anything he'd gained?

✦ We've considered what the Preacher reveals about his heart—what motivated his pursuits—but let's look a bit more closely at the things in which he sought pleasure. As you read back through verses 1–11, where do you see blatant sin, concrete violations of God's command to love him supremely and to love one's neighbor?

4. LIGHT—OR DARKNESS? (2:12-17)

Having obtained everything a powerful king could enjoy, and recognizing in the process that success and pleasure aren't the keys to a meaningful life, the Preacher considers whether wisdom is really more worthwhile than folly or foolishness:

> ^{12} So I turned to consider wisdom and madness and folly. For what can the man do who comes after the king? Only what has already been done. ^{13} Then I saw that there is more gain in wisdom than in folly, as there is more gain in light than in darkness. ^{14} The wise person has his eyes in his head, but the fool walks in darkness. And yet I perceived that the same event happens to all of them. ^{15} Then I said in my heart, "What happens to the fool will happen to me also. Why then have I been so very wise?" And I said in my heart that this also is vanity. ^{16} For of the wise as of the fool there is no enduring remembrance, seeing that in the days to come all will have been long forgotten. How the wise dies just like the fool! ^{17} So I hated life, because what is done under the sun was grievous to me, for all is vanity and a striving after wind. (vv. 12–17)

The Preacher concludes that wisdom is better than folly, just as light is more beneficial than darkness. Use the "Light and Darkness" chart that follows to get a glimpse of why light and darkness are good ways to distinguish between wisdom and folly. Note what is held out as light and, conversely, what breeds darkness. Summarize your findings in the space provided below the chart.

Light and Darkness		
	Source of Light and Where It Leads	Source of Darkness and Where It Leads
Psalm 119:105		
Proverbs 4:19		

Light and Darkness		
	Source of Light and Where It Leads	Source of Darkness and Where It Leads
John 8:12		
Ephesians 5:8–11		
1 Thessalonians 5:1–11		
1 John 2:9–11		

· Summary:

....

....

....

✦ The Preacher concludes in verse 13 that wisdom is indeed better than folly, so why does he say, in verses 14–16, that this truth doesn't satisfy the hunger underlying his quest?

....

....

....

....

After his investigation of wisdom and folly, the Preacher declares that he hates life (v. 17). It's hard to know what to make of such a discouraging remark. Later, in 9:4–5, he states that life is preferable to death, so we can conclude that actual hatred here in verse 17 is unlikely. It's best to take the "hatred" here as a literary way of emphasizing his primary point: despite his vast wisdom, his ending is no different from the fool's.

5. HARD LABOR (2:18-23)

The Preacher now concludes that all his work is no better than all his wisdom:

> ¹⁸ I hated all my toil in which I toil under the sun, seeing that I must leave it to the man who will come after me, ¹⁹ and who knows whether he will be wise or a fool? Yet he will be master of all for which I toiled and used my wisdom under the sun. This also is vanity. ²⁰ So I turned about and gave my heart up to despair over all the toil of my labors under the sun, ²¹ because sometimes a person who has toiled with wisdom and knowledge and skill must leave everything to be enjoyed by someone who did not toil for it. This also is vanity and a great evil. ²² What has a man from all the toil and striving of heart with which he toils beneath the sun? ²³ For all his days are full of sorrow, and his work is a vexation. Even in the night his heart does not rest. This also is vanity. (vv. 18–23)

✦ In verse 18 the Preacher expresses the same sort of hatred toward his work as he did toward life in general. What reason does he give in verses 19–21 for his negative outlook?

_____

_____

_____

The Preacher concludes in verse 23 that life is "full of sorrow" and that "work is a vexation." Perhaps you are nodding along in agreement and asking yourself, *Why would God allow this to be true?* We can make sense of this grim perspective by going back once again to the beginning of the Bible, to Genesis 3, where we're told that Adam and Eve disobeyed God. Afterward God told them the consequences of their sin, and from this we can understand why life and work are so hard.

✤ Read Genesis 3:17–19 (we looked at this passage in Week 1, but consider it again here in light of Ecclesiastes 2:18–23). How do the Lord's words to Adam explain the Preacher's conclusions about life?

6. PATHWAY TO PLEASURE (2:24-26)

Notice the subtle shift in the Preacher's perspective when he sees God as overarching all of life:

> ²⁴There is nothing better for a person than that he should eat and drink and find enjoyment in his toil. This also, I saw, is from the hand of God, ²⁵for apart from him who can eat or who can have enjoyment? ²⁶For to the one who pleases him God has given wisdom and knowledge and joy, but to the sinner he has given the business of gathering and collecting, only to give to one who pleases God. This also is vanity and a striving after wind. (vv. 24–26)

At first glance, his words about eating and drinking might seem like nothing more than a prescription for coping with the hardships of life, but his subsequent words reveal a much deeper meaning. He's actually saying something vitally significant here, which is that wisdom and work and all of life's pleasures are meant to bring joy and meaning when God is recognized and acknowledged as the source of those things. If we live our lives oriented toward God—if everything we do is anchored in God's word and ways—we will find fulfillment. And it's the *only* way to find it in this sin-cursed world.

The Preacher then distinguishes between the blessings experienced by one who pleases God and "the sinner" who doesn't in verse 26. He's not implying that people can earn God's blessings by achieving some level of sinlessness. If that were the case, no one would ever be blessed since everyone is a sinner! We can understand verse 26 when we recognize it as *wisdom* language. Remember that the Bible's Wisdom Books make astute observations about how God has designed the world to work. We see this especially in Proverbs. Wisdom language shows us that, in general, those who live God-centered lives—what the Wisdom Books call living in "the fear of the Lord"—experience the

---

The "Fear of the Lord" in Biblical Wisdom

- The fear of the Lord is wisdom (Job 28:28; Psalm 111:10; Proverbs 9:10; 15:33).
- The fear of the Lord is pure (Psalm 19:9).
- The fear of the Lord is knowledge (Proverbs 1:7).
- The fear of the Lord is a choice (Proverbs 1:29).
- The fear of the Lord is hatred of evil (Proverbs 8:13).
- The fear of the Lord brings life (Proverbs 10:27; 14:27; 19:23; 22:4).
- The fear of the Lord imparts confidence (Proverbs 14:26).
- The fear of the Lord produces repentance (Proverbs 16:6).
- The fear of the Lord is satisfying (Proverbs 19:23).
- The fear of the Lord is security (Proverbs 19:23; Ecclesiastes 7:18; 8:12).
- The fear of the Lord brings blessing (Psalms 34:9; 112:1; 115:13; 128:1; Proverbs 22:4; 28:14).
- The fear of the Lord provides guidance (Psalms 25:12).
- The fear of the Lord is righteousness (Proverbs 14:2).

---

blessings that accompany righteousness, while those who disregard him taste the consequences of living outside the paths of blessing. The refrain at the end, that "this also is vanity and a striving after wind" (v. 26), drives home the point that human beings cannot set the terms for when, where, and how they experience life's blessings.

LET'S TALK

1. Excess ruins enjoyment, whatever the indulgence. The Bible makes this point in both Old and New Testaments. When and how have you experienced this truth for yourself? Look at Galatians 5:19–24. How can this passage shape your view of the things you choose to indulge in?

....

....

....

2. The Preacher reflects, "There is nothing better for a person than that he should eat and drink and find enjoyment in his toil. This also, I saw, is from the hand of God" (2:24). Talk about how the simple things of day-to-day life can be experienced with joy rather than with a depressing sense of futility. You might want to include 1 Timothy 6:17 in your discussion.

....

....

....

....

....

....

....

....

....

A TIME, A PLACE, AND AN ULTIMATE PURPOSE

ECCLESIASTES 3:1-22

You didn't have to grow up in the 1960s to recognize The Byrd's hit song "Turn! Turn! Turn!" when you hear it. What most people don't know is that the lyrics are an adaptation of the Preacher's (arguably more famous) poem in Ecclesiastes 3. This hauntingly beautiful poem outlines the normal course of life and the way it's lived, but the effect of the poem is to point us beyond our lives to something else, as we will see. The Preacher gives more reflections on toil—what we more readily refer to as "labor" or "work"—and we'll also get some of his reflections on the evil of injustice. Primarily, though, the Preacher has a lot to say about God in this chapter. He shows us the God who beautifies, the God who seeks, the God who tests, and the God who determines every beginning and every ending.

1. A TIME FOR—EVERYTHING (3:1-8)

Every person, plan, and purpose has a set time, the Preacher tells us. Although we live this reality daily, we don't consciously think about it in the way he sets out in this poetic passage:

> ¹For everything there is a season, and a time for every matter under heaven:
>
> ² a time to be born, and a time to die;
>> a time to plant, and a time to pluck up what is planted;

³   a time to kill, and a time to heal;
     a time to break down, and a time to build up;
⁴   a time to weep, and a time to laugh;
     a time to mourn, and a time to dance;
⁵   a time to cast away stones, and a time to gather stones together;
     a time to embrace, and a time to refrain from embracing;
⁶   a time to seek, and a time to lose;
     a time to keep, and a time to cast away;
⁷   a time to tear, and a time to sew;
     a time to keep silence, and a time to speak;
⁸   a time to love, and a time to hate;
     a time for war, and a time for peace. (vv. 1–8)

✦ We don't need to make an application from the individual "time" components in the poem. Instead, we should view it as a whole, the range of what happens to everyone over the course of a lifetime. What do you think the Preacher is conveying in his poem?

✦ Read Psalm 107. What does the psalm teach us about God's role in life's various ups and downs and how to respond to God as we live in the midst of them?

2. A TIME FOR BEAUTY (3:9–14)

"What gain has the worker from his toil?" The Preacher has addressed this issue before, and he concluded that since we all end up in the exact same condition, no matter our accomplishments, our labors aren't what give life meaning (2:18–21). Here, in chapter 3, he shows us what does:

> ⁹ What gain has the worker from his toil? ¹⁰ I have seen the business that God has given to the children of man to be busy with. ¹¹ He has made everything beautiful in its time. Also, he has put eternity into man's heart, yet so that he cannot find out what God has done from the beginning to the end. ¹² I perceived that there is nothing better for them than to be joyful and to do good as long as they live; ¹³ also that everyone should eat and drink and take pleasure in all his toil—this is God's gift to man.
>
> ¹⁴ I perceived that whatever God does endures forever; nothing can be added to it, nor anything taken from it. God has done it, so that people fear before him. (vv. 9–14).

🕊 In order to make sense of our times and seasons, the Preacher shows us life from God's perspective. From this passage, note what he has observed about God's ways and purposes:

- "I have seen" (v. 10):

- "I perceived" (v. 12):

- "I perceived" (v. 14):

✤ How do God's purposes as seen here in verses 9–14 help you make sense of the poem in verses 1–8?

....

....

....

....

> *"In what you see, what you hear, and what*
> *you do—take joy! Reminders of our mortality*
> *should motivate us to rejoice."*[10]

✤ The Preacher writes that God "has made everything beautiful in its time" (v. 11). What do Isaiah 61:1–11 and Ephesians 1:3–10 unveil about the ultimate meaning of the Preacher's words here?

....

....

....

....

3. THE GOD WHO SEEKS (3:15)

Before he switches gears a bit, the Preacher adds one more thing that God does:

> [15] That which is, already has been; that which is to be, already has been; and God seeks what has been driven away. (v. 15)

✤ Read Genesis 3:22–24 together with Revelation 22:1–5. How do these passages provide deep meaning to what the Preacher writes here in verse 15?

....

....

4. UPSIDE-DOWN WORLD (3:16-17)

In our fallen world, evil finds a way into everything, from law courts to God's house, which, in Solomon's day, was the temple. Here's how the Preacher describes it:

> ¹⁶ Moreover, I saw under the sun that in the place of justice, even there was wickedness, and in the place of righteousness, even there was wickedness. ¹⁷ I said in my heart, God will judge the righteous and the wicked, for there is a time for every matter and for every work. (vv. 16–17)

✦ What a somber observation we're given in verses 16–17! Even so, there's encouragement here for God's people. What hope is held out to believers in verse 17 in the midst of evil happenings?

5. THE GOD WHO TESTS (3:18-22)

One of the most heart-wrenching moments at a graveside funeral is when the minister intones, "Ashes to ashes, dust to dust . . ." Those words come from what God said to Adam after his fall into sin: "By the sweat of your face you shall eat bread, till you return to the ground, for out of it you were taken; for you are dust, and to dust you shall return" (Genesis 3:19). The Preacher reflects on this sad consequence:

> ¹⁸ I said in my heart with regard to the children of man that God is testing them that they may see that they themselves are but beasts. ¹⁹ For what happens to the children of man and what happens to the beasts is the same; as one dies, so dies the other. They all have the same breath, and man has no advantage over the beasts, for all is vanity. ²⁰ All go to one place. All are from the dust, and to dust all return. ²¹ Who knows whether the spirit of man goes upward and the spirit of the beast goes down into the earth? ²² So I saw that there is nothing better than

that a man should rejoice in his work, for that is his lot. Who can bring him to see what will be after him? (vv. 18–22)

God's testing of human beings isn't the kind of test our teachers give us in school to reveal how well we've learned a particular subject. The test of verse 18 is actually designed to teach us something that we have *not* learned! God wants us to see that we are like beasts in our fallenness. No matter how much we accomplish with our skills and resources, we end up dying just like animals and are incapable of comprehending spiritual realities. So, he says, take pleasure in and rejoice in the work you do—something animals cannot do. "Both animals and humans can work, but only humans can enjoy their work and the results of their labors."[11]

✝ So death is the reality for everyone. But for those who are born again, united to Christ by faith, there is a radically different outcome. Life in Christ far exceeds the enjoyment of earthly blessings. In Christ our labors—and, yes, even the difficulties we experience in a fallen world—have eternal value and purpose. Keeping in mind the Preacher's description of fallen humans in verses 18–22, how do the following passages reveal what's different for those who are born again in Christ?

· John 14:1–3

· Romans 8:18–25

· 1 Peter 1:3–4

LET'S TALK

1. The Preacher's poem in 3:2–8 gives us something concrete to replace the trite slogans we hear in a crisis: "It'll all work out" (sometimes it doesn't, right?) or "You got this!" (No, actually, we don't, but God does). Discuss how the poem reshapes your perspective on the various ups and downs you experience, and perhaps even a current difficulty.

2. The truth is that for those who trust in Christ for salvation, all troubles end with this life, but for those who reject him, their experiences here are as good as it will ever be. Ecclesiastes 3 gives us some powerful insights into the lives of unbelievers (which includes our unsaved loved ones)—what they see and know and are blind to. Consider how these insights can better equip you to share your faith.

SOMETHING BETTER

ECCLESIASTES 4:1-16

God created us to belong. Whatever we do, wherever we do it, and whomever we do it with—we thrive on collaboration, to be included when plans are crafted, decisions are made, and insider knowledge is traded. We want a place at the table, a reserved seat. Once seated, however, if our personal preferences and contributions aren't valued as highly as we'd like, we might grow impatient and discontented with our seat assignment, and begin angling for a more prominent place. We all sit at collaborative "tables" of one sort or another—social media tables, career tables, student tables, ministry tables. Whatever our personal "table," we want our voice to count. We want to be noticed and, if we're honest, *honored*. The craving for honor crushes love and breeds envy and ultimately gets us nowhere. The Preacher exposes some of these ugly heart motives this week along with the dangers they pose, and then he shows us collaboration that's live-giving rather than life-taking.

1. BEATEN DOWN (4:1-3)

In his quest to understand life in a fallen world, the Preacher observed something so grim, so depressingly bleak, that, for a season, he despaired of life itself:

> ¹Again I saw all the oppressions that are done under the sun. And behold, the tears of the oppressed, and they had no one to comfort them! On the side of their oppressors there was power, and there was no one to comfort them! ²And I thought the dead who are already dead more fortunate than the living who are

still alive. ³ But better than both is he who has not yet been and has not seen the evil deeds that are done under the sun. (vv. 1–3)

What picture does the Preacher give of both the oppressed and those who oppress them?

· The oppressed:

· The oppressors:

Power can be used for good, but so often in our sin-scarred world it is used for selfish, evil purposes. Identify some of the ways people typically achieve power.

The Preacher despairs over the plight of the oppressed, how helpless and alone they are. Their plight troubles him so much that he repeats his lament: there is "no one to comfort them" (v. 1). Oppression is just as prevalent in our day and age because sin is just as prevalent, but we don't have to adopt a grim outlook on life. How do the following passages show us a better way to deal with the oppression we see—and perhaps even experience?

· Psalm 9:9–10

....

....

....

· Psalm 103:6

....

....

....

· 1 Corinthians 1:26–29

....

....

....

· 2 Corinthians 1:3–5

....

....

....

2. THE EVIL OF ENVY (4:4-6)

In his quest for understanding, the Preacher has picked up a good bit about human nature:

> [4] Then I saw that all toil and all skill in work come from a man's envy of his neighbor. This also is vanity and a striving after wind.
> [5] The fool folds his hands and eats his own flesh.
> [6] Better is a handful of quietness than two hands full of toil and a striving after wind. (vv. 4–6)

Envy rises from our fallen nature. Jesus listed the kinds of sins that originate in the heart, and he included envy on that list (Mark 7:21–23). Jesus's point is that envy doesn't come from our lacking something someone else has but from what our heart most wants. Envy is a powerful poison—so much so that it motivated the chief priests to deliver Jesus over for crucifixion (Mark 15:10). Also Proverbs 14:30 tells us that "envy makes the bones rot."

✦ How does the Preacher link envy to the work people do and the way they do it?

✦ If envy is a futile reason for work, refusing to work is not the antidote. How does the Preacher make this point in his description of the fool in verse 5?

> "The universe you inhabit and the life you have today
> come from God's hand as something you do not deserve.
> Your life is on loan for a short while, and one day God
> will call time and take it back. . . . So embrace life for
> what it is rather than what you'd like it to be."[12]

✦ Better than hard work fueled by envy ("two hands full of toil and a striving after wind") —or refusing to work at all—is "a handful of quietness" (v. 6). The Preacher uses the image of hands to contrast two very different lifestyles. What point do you think he is making?

....

....

....

....

3. ALONE AT THE TOP (4:7-8)

The privileges and pitfalls of work are still on the Preacher's mind as he continues:

> [7] Again, I saw vanity under the sun: [8] one person who has no other, either son or brother, yet there is no end to all his toil, and his eyes are never satisfied with riches, so that he never asks, "For whom am I toiling and depriving myself of pleasure?" This also is vanity and an unhappy business. (vv. 7–8)

If you're familiar with Charles Dickens's *A Christmas Carol*, you'll recognize that Ebenezer Scrooge is an ideal fictional embodiment of what we read in verses 7–8. Mr. Scrooge, a businessman who lived for money, is described in Dickens's story as "a squeezing, wrenching, grasping, scraping, clutching, covetous, old sinner! Hard and sharp as flint . . . secret, and self-contained, and solitary as an oyster."[13] The story has a redemptive ending, but until then, Ebenezer is made to see the personal cost of his greed.

✦ What do the following passages show us about a godly approach to wealth?

· Philippians 4:11–13

....

....

....

· Colossians 3:23–24

....

....

....

· 1 Timothy 6:6–10

· Hebrews 13:5–6

· 1 John 2:15–17

4. WHEN MORE IS BETTER (4:9-12)

In 2023 the surgeon general of the United States concluded that "the mortality impact of being socially disconnected is similar to that caused by smoking up to 15 cigarettes a day."[14] Unlike the surgeon general, the Preacher in Ecclesiastes didn't have access to medical science data, but his writing, after all, was inspired by God, which led him to a similar conclusion:

> [9] Two are better than one, because they have a good reward for their toil. [10] For if they fall, one will lift up his fellow. But woe to him who is alone when he falls and has not another to lift him up! [11] Again, if two lie together, they keep warm, but how can one keep warm alone? [12] And though a man might prevail against one who is alone, two will withstand him—a threefold cord is not quickly broken. (vv. 9–12)

The Preacher's words here are often cited at weddings, and while the passage is certainly fitting at a marriage ceremony, it is not what the Preacher had in mind. The context here is work—labor and toil. There were significant dangers for laborers in ancient Israel as they traveled and moved about, including intense weather conditions, crime, and risk to life and limb. For that reason, it was safer for two or even three people to work together.

Most of us don't face those same dangers in our jobs today, but some do. Either way, we can broaden the application of the Preacher's words to simply living life with other believers. How is this shown in the following passages?

· 1 Corinthians 12:12–26

· Hebrews 10:24–25

"Fellowship is more than sharing a cup of coffee after the service; it is sharing life together—sharing sorrows, fears, and pains—so that together we might fight the good fight, finish the race, keep the faith, and long for the glory of Christ's appearing."[15]

5. DOWN AND UP AND BACK AGAIN (4:13–16)

Next, the Preacher gives us a rags-to-riches story:

[13] Better was a poor and wise youth than an old and foolish king who no longer knew how to take advice. [14] For he went from prison to the throne, though in his own kingdom he had been born poor. [15] I saw all the living who move about

under the sun, along with that youth who was to stand in the king's place. [16] There was no end of all the people, all of whom he led. Yet those who come later will not rejoice in him. Surely this also is vanity and a striving after wind. (vv. 13–16)

What is the point of the Preacher's story?

....

....

....

....

LET'S TALK

1. Do we share the Preacher's indignation at the oppression we see, the abuses of power we witness and read about? Discuss how you tend to respond when you see it. What sort of abuses do you ignore or avoid or, on the other hand, proactively seek to remedy? What makes the difference for you? If you have been victimized or oppressed, what in this week's lesson can guide and shape your response from this point forward?

....

....

....

....

....

....

....

2. Everyone struggles with envy. It's woven into our fallen nature. Talk about the particular occasions, relationships, or situations that can ignite envy in your heart. Share how you tend to respond and how those responses have impacted the situations that provoked the envy in the first place.

WHAT DO YOU LIVE FOR?

ECCLESIASTES 5:1-6:12

What do you live for? Everyone lives for something. It's easy enough to rattle off the "right" answer, but it's worth considering whether our deeds and decisions match our words. We seek to please God, but are we motivated more by desire for his gifts than desire for him? We agree with God's word that wealth doesn't guarantee security, but are we often controlled by money anxieties? As Christ followers we claim that power and prestige are unworthy pursuits, but are we overly focused on accumulating social media likes? To put it in the Preacher's terms, does wisdom—orienting our lives around God, his word and ways—determine not only what we say but all we do as well? We can use these questions as a diagnostic tool for our hearts as we study the material in this week's lesson. The Preacher shows us that our concept of God is crucial because how we view him determines how we worship him. We're also going to see (again!) that since wealth never delivers what it promises, it's pointless to devote ourselves to acquiring more and more. Surprisingly, a primary emphasis this week is *enjoyment*. We're going to see a great paradox: enjoyment of life's blessings comes not from those actual blessings but from the God who gives them.

1. YOUR MOUTH MATTERS (5:1-7)

God delights when we worship him, and he cares *how* we worship him too. His great love for us ought to inspire awe-filled praise rather than casual irreverence. Worship that befits an awesome God is what the Preacher has in mind here:

¹Guard your steps when you go to the house of God. To draw near to listen is better than to offer the sacrifice of fools, for they do not know that they are doing evil. ²Be not rash with your mouth, nor let your heart be hasty to utter a word before God, for God is in heaven and you are on earth. Therefore let your words be few. ³For a dream comes with much business, and a fool's voice with many words.

⁴When you vow a vow to God, do not delay paying it, for he has no pleasure in fools. Pay what you vow. ⁵It is better that you should not vow than that you should vow and not pay. ⁶Let not your mouth lead you into sin, and do not say before the messenger that it was a mistake. Why should God be angry at your voice and destroy the work of your hands? ⁷For when dreams increase and words grow many, there is vanity; but God is the one you must fear. (5:1–7)

> *"Do not work for the food that perishes, but for the food that endures to eternal life, which the Son of Man will give to you. For on him God the Father has set his seal." (John 6:27)*

✦ What do people's words convey about their worship?

_____

_____

_____

_____

✦ Under the old covenant, before Christ came, God's people brought sacrifices to the temple as part of their worship, but as with any worship practice, it was meant to be offered from the heart. Just going through the motions isn't actually worship, which is why the Preacher writes in 5:1, "To draw near to listen is better than to offer the sacrifice of fools, for they do not know that they are doing evil." How does Micah 6:6–8 help us understand what the Preacher means here?

_____

_____

We see a good bit about vows in this passage. Making vows was not uncommon in ancient Israel. Both men and women could make vows before the Lord. One such vow, called the "Nazarite vow," was a way of separating oneself to the Lord for a set time period. For the duration of the vow, no alcohol was consumed, hair was grown long, and dead bodies were to be avoided, even if the deceased was a close family member. (To learn more about the Nazarite vow, read Numbers 6:1–21.) There is also the story of Hannah, who vowed that if the Lord would enable her to conceive a child, she would dedicate that child to the Lord's service for life (1 Samuel 1:1–28).

✦ Look again at what the Preacher says about vows here in Ecclesiastes 5:1–7. In particular, he warns against making a rash or impulsive vow, promise, or commitment before God. Why do you think the Preacher calls hasty vow-makers "fools"?

2. BITTER OR SWEET? (5:8–12)

After noting again in 5:8–9 that the poor are treated unfairly by the powerful, he offers more wisdom about wealth in 5:10–12:

> [8] If you see in a province the oppression of the poor and the violation of justice and righteousness, do not be amazed at the matter, for the high official is watched by a higher, and there are yet higher ones over them. [9] But this is gain for a land in every way: a king committed to cultivated fields.
> [10] He who loves money will not be satisfied with money, nor he who loves wealth with his income; this also is vanity. [11] When goods increase, they increase who eat them, and what advantage has their owner but to see them with his eyes? [12] Sweet is the sleep of a laborer, whether he eats little or much, but the full stomach of the rich will not let him sleep. (5:8–12)

In Week 4, we noted that wealth doesn't bring contentment. In fact, as we saw, seeking satisfaction in money, what the apostle Paul calls "the love of money," underlies much evil, and those who pursue it are in danger of wandering away from the faith and into many sorrows (1 Timothy 6:9–10). The Preacher emphasizes that idea here in 5:10, and then he goes on to describe the *futility* of wealth as a means of ease, peace, and comfort.

✦ What do Jesus's words in Matthew 6:19–24 build on the Preacher's observations?

✦ The proverb in Ecclesiastes 5:12 tells us, "Sweet is the sleep of a laborer, whether he eats little or much, but the full stomach of the rich will not let him sleep." The point is that those who live for money and what it can buy won't find satisfaction in those things. According to the following passages, what is the source of sleep that is "sweet"?

· Psalm 4:8

· Psalm 121:4

· Psalm 127:2

· Proverbs 3:24–26

3. WISDOM AND WEALTH (5:13–17)

Still on the topic of wealth, the Preacher paints another scenario, this time focusing on the "grievous evil" of hoarding money:

> [13] There is a grievous evil that I have seen under the sun: riches were kept by their owner to his hurt, [14] and those riches were lost in a bad venture. And he is father of a son, but he has nothing in his hand. [15] As he came from his mother's womb he shall go again, naked as he came, and shall take nothing for his toil that he may carry away in his hand. [16] This also is a grievous evil: just as he came, so shall he go, and what gain is there to him who toils for the wind? [17] Moreover, all his days he eats in darkness in much vexation and sickness and anger. (5:13–17)

🕊 Summarize in your own words what the Preacher says about the futility of hoarding our personal assets. (If you have a few extra minutes, read Jesus's parable of the rich fool in Luke 12:13–21.)

4. A GIFT FROM GOD (5:18–20)

In contrast to what is grievous and evil, the Preacher remarks on what he has observed to be "good and fitting":

> [18] Behold, what I have seen to be good and fitting is to eat and drink and find enjoyment in all the toil with which one toils under the sun the few days of his life that God has given him, for this is his lot. [19] Everyone also to whom God has given wealth and possessions and power to enjoy them, and to accept his lot and

rejoice in his toil—this is the gift of God. ²⁰ For he will not much remember the days of his life because God keeps him occupied with joy in his heart. (5:18–20)

✦ The Preacher said something very similar back in 2:24–26. What specific gifts from God can you identify in that passage?

....

....

....

....

5. THE PLEASURE PRINCIPLE (6:1-9)

In contrast to those who enjoy the fruits of their labors as God's gift are those who cannot enjoy those fruits:

> ¹ There is an evil that I have seen under the sun, and it lies heavy on mankind: ² a man to whom God gives wealth, possessions, and honor, so that he lacks nothing of all that he desires, yet God does not give him power to enjoy them, but a stranger enjoys them. This is vanity; it is a grievous evil. ³ If a man fathers a hundred children and lives many years, so that the days of his years are many, but his soul is not satisfied with life's good things, and he also has no burial, I say that a stillborn child is better off than he. ⁴ For it comes in vanity and goes in darkness, and in darkness its name is covered. ⁵ Moreover, it has not seen the sun or known anything, yet it finds rest rather than he. ⁶ Even though he should live a thousand years twice over, yet enjoy no good—do not all go to the one place? (6:1–6)

✦ How does the Preacher view someone who cannot enjoy life's good things?

....

....

....

....

The Preacher continues with the same theme:

> [7] All the toil of man is for his mouth, yet his appetite is not satisfied. [8] For what advantage has the wise man over the fool? And what does the poor man have who knows how to conduct himself before the living? [9] Better is the sight of the eyes than the wandering of the appetite: this also is vanity and a striving after wind. (6:7–9)

🕊 As you look at this passage as a whole, what do you think is the meaning of the Preacher's proverb, "Better is the sight of the eyes than the wandering of the appetite"—in 6:9?

Chapter 6 concludes with some questions:

> [10] Whatever has come to be has already been named, and it is known what man is, and that he is not able to dispute with one stronger than he. [11] The more words, the more vanity, and what is the advantage to man? [12] For who knows what is good for man while he lives the few days of his vain life, which he passes like a shadow? For who can tell man what will be after him under the sun? (6:10–12)

How would you answer the Preacher's questions? Give it some thought as you wrap up this section. We'll get the Preacher's answers in next week's lesson.

> *"It is not merely that money can't buy joy;*
> *it is also that God makes sure of it."*[16]

LET'S TALK

1. God is worthy of our worship, and that includes the way we worship. What is the essence of reverent worship, and how is it offered in practice? Discuss the worship styles you've observed or participated in. What about the music or liturgy or other aspects of a worship service make those services reverent or irreverent?

2. The more we have, the more there is to maintain. A bigger house means more cleaning, more furnishing, more insuring. A large yard requires landscaping. The Preacher describes it this way: "When goods increase, they increase who eat them, and what advantage has their owner but to see them with his eyes?" (5:11). How have you experienced this in your own life with your own material means?

PLAYING THE LONG GAME

ECCLESIASTES 7:1-29

While in the fictional world of Narnia, Lucy Pevensie finds a magician's book of spells, one of which gives her the ability to hear what her friends are saying about her in places far away. Lucy reads the magic spell and becomes upset when she overhears a friend betray her. Aslan comes to Lucy and says, "I think you have been eavesdropping. . . . And you have misjudged your friend. She is weak, but she loves you. She was afraid of the older girl and said what she does not mean." Lucy tells Aslan, "I don't think I'd ever be able to forget what I heard her say," and Aslan replies, "No, you won't."[17] In Ecclesiastes 7, in one of a series of proverbs, the Preacher cautions against this very sort of unwise listening. He also leads us to consider the reality of death. We're going to see more of this theme as we work our way through the rest of the book. No one likes to think about death, and it's considered an inappropriate topic at social occasions. Today we attend "celebrations of life" rather than funerals or memorial services. Facing the reality of death is wise, the Preacher tells us, and we will explore why this week. We'll also focus on the wisdom of patience—a virtue often forgotten in our instant age.

1. REMEMBER DEATH (7:1-4)

Death can't help but make us think deeply about what really matters. It reframes our perspective when we're so caught up in the stresses and inconveniences of day-to-day life that we lose sight of the big, eternal picture. Everything in our world gets reoriented when a loved one dies—or when we face our own deaths. The Preacher guides us how to process times like these:

> 1   A good name is better than precious ointment,
>   and the day of death than the day of birth.
> 2   It is better to go to the house of mourning
>   than to go to the house of feasting,
>   for this is the end of all mankind,
>   and the living will lay it to heart.
> 3   Sorrow is better than laughter,
>   for by sadness of face the heart is made glad.
> 4   The heart of the wise is in the house of mourning,
>   but the heart of fools is in the house of mirth. (vv. 1–4)

✦ The way someone lives will impact how she is remembered. How is this pictured in verse 1?

....

....

....

....

The Preacher tells us that facing death has benefits. The "day of death" that he described as "better" in verse 1 isn't our own death but that of someone else. His point is that death makes us stop and think about how we are living in light of our own inevitable death. Will we leave a good name, and if so, in what way? That is the point of all his "better" statements in this passage.

✦ How do Jesus's words in Matthew 5:2–4 take us deeper into the Preacher's point here?

....

....

....

✦ A primary focus this week is the contrast between wisdom and folly. We find the first instance in verse 4. We've already seen why time in "the house of mourning" is wise, so, in light of this, what do you think he means when he says that "the heart of fools is in the house of mirth" (v. 4)?

> *"Believers are called to follow Christ, in whom all the treasures of wisdom and knowledge are found (Col. 2:3). The pervasiveness of sin is finally dealt with only on the cross, as Christ became sin for us so that we might become 'the righteousness of God.'"*[18]

2. BEWARE SONGS AND LAUGHTER (7:5-6)

Wise people are those who discern what's best, unlike fools who live impulsively and pursue nothing more than feel-good-in-the-moment gratification:

> 5 It is better for a man to hear the rebuke of the wise
> than to hear the song of fools.
> 6 For as the crackling of thorns under a pot,
> so is the laughter of the fools;
> this also is vanity. (vv. 5–6)

✦ Why do you think it is better to listen to a wise rebuke than the song of a fool?

✦ Thorns crackling under a pot—what a vivid image! When we want a good, roaring fire, we use sturdy logs, not thorn branches. What point is the Preacher making about fools here in verse 6?

....

....

....

....

3. EASY DOES IT (7:7–9)

The next few proverbs show the wisdom of responding patiently to various challenges:

> ⁷ Surely oppression drives the wise into madness,
>   and a bribe corrupts the heart.
> ⁸ Better is the end of a thing than its beginning,
>   and the patient in spirit is better than the proud in spirit.
> ⁹ Be not quick in your spirit to become angry,
>   for anger lodges in the heart of fools. (vv. 7–9)

It makes sense to see the "oppression" in verse 7 as financial oppression, since money is clearly in view when he speaks of bribes. Again we see the power of wealth, here in its ability to tempt someone to sin, whether to make a foolish, rash decision to escape oppression or to sin willfully for financial gain. In the same way that the bribe of verse 7 helps us understand the kind of oppression the Preacher has in mind, "patient in spirit" in the second part of verse 8 sheds light on "the end of a thing is better than its beginning" in the first part. The point is, "to see a project through to its end is better than to be the kind of person who starts and never finishes. . . . Anything worthwhile takes time to develop and grow, so give it the time it needs."[19]

✦ The Preacher next makes a connection between impatience and anger, a connection we find repeatedly in the Bible's Wisdom Books, especially Proverbs. Why do you think impatience and anger are linked? Fill in the "Effects of Anger and Patience" chart on the next page to shape your answer.

Effects of Anger and Patience		
	Effects of Anger	Effects of Patience
Proverbs 14:29		
Proverbs 15:18		
Proverbs 16:32		

4. THAT WAS THEN, THIS IS NOW (7:10-14)

Next we are guided how to respond wisely to life's various changes and seasons:

> ¹⁰ Say not, "Why were the former days better than these?"
>   For it is not from wisdom that you ask this.
> ¹¹ Wisdom is good with an inheritance,
>   an advantage to those who see the sun.
> ¹² For the protection of wisdom is like the protection of money,
>   and the advantage of knowledge is that wisdom preserves the life of
>   him who has it.
> ¹³ Consider the work of God:
>   who can make straight what he has made crooked?

¹⁴ In the day of prosperity be joyful, and in the day of adversity consider: God has made the one as well as the other, so that man may not find out anything that will be after him. (vv. 10–14)

Photo albums are largely a thing of the past in our advanced digital age, but capturing life's meaningful moments in pictures is still very much part of our lives. It's fun to look back on important occasions, and photos help us to remember the details. But this is not the kind of looking back that the Preacher has in mind when he speaks about "former days" in verse 10. He's talking about nostalgia. We tend to think of nostalgia as something nice—fond memories of good times—but nostalgia has a dark side. It's more than a fond memory—it's memory with the reality stripped out. Nostalgia is *selective* memory, and it's rarely accurate.

✦ The root of nostalgia is *longing*, a desire for something once enjoyed but now lost. Why do you think indulging in nostalgia is unwise?

✦ The Preacher has been quick to point out the dangers of wealth, but in verse 12 he is also realistic about its advantages. How does he link wisdom and wealth in verses 11–12?

✦ What does the Preacher convey about God in verses 13–14 and thus about us and our very own lives?

5. A WELL-MEASURED LIFE (7:15–18)

When the Preacher describes his life as "vain" in verse 15, he isn't speaking of its worth. Rather, wisdom has enabled him to recognize that his life, like everyone's, passes quickly. He continues to share what he's observed in his quest to understand life in a fallen world:

> [15] In my vain life I have seen everything. There is a righteous man who perishes in his righteousness, and there is a wicked man who prolongs his life in his evildoing. [16] Be not overly righteous, and do not make yourself too wise. Why should you destroy yourself? [17] Be not overly wicked, neither be a fool. Why should you die before your time? [18] It is good that you should take hold of this, and from that withhold not your hand, for the one who fears God shall come out from both of them. (vv. 15–18)

We can't help but do a double-take at the Preacher's instruction, "Be not overly righteous, and do not make yourself too wise" (v. 16). His words seem to contradict everything he's written until now. Bible scholar Doug O'Donnell sheds some helpful light on these baffling words: "The sense is this: If anyone—whether righteous or unrighteous—can die young (which, of course, is true), then do not think that somehow obtaining ultra-righteousness will be an absolute insurance against such calamity."[20] At the same time, the Bible's Wisdom Books reveal that God has hardwired the world such that those who are wise generally prosper in this life, and those who are fools do not.

Since we ultimately have no control over our destiny, how, according to this passage, should we orient our thinking and living?

_____

_____

_____

6. WISE ASSESSMENT (7:19–22)

The Preacher adds a few more observations:

> [19] Wisdom gives strength to the wise man more than ten rulers who are in a city. [20] Surely there is not a righteous man on earth who does good and never sins. [21] Do not take to heart all the things that people say, lest you hear your servant cursing you. [22] Your heart knows that many times you yourself have cursed others. (vv. 19–22)

✤ What do these verses teach you about:

· Wisdom:

....

....

....

· Sin:

....

....

....

· Yourself:

....

....

....

✤ Verse 20 exposes our greatest problem—"Surely there is not a righteous man on earth who does good and never sins"—and therefore our greatest need. How does Romans 3:23–26 reveal what this verse points us to?

....

....

....

....

7. WHERE KNOWLEDGE LEADS (7:23-29)

When I was twenty, I thought I knew everything. When I was thirty, I realized there were lots of things I didn't know. And when I turned forty, I realized I actually knew very little. No doubt the same is true for you, however many years you've lived. With knowledge comes the realization of how little knowledge we actually possess:

²³ All this I have tested by wisdom. I said, "I will be wise," but it was far from me. ²⁴ That which has been is far off, and deep, very deep; who can find it out? (vv. 23–24)

In his determination to know and understand, the Preacher tells us more of what he found:

²⁵ I turned my heart to know and to search out and to seek wisdom and the scheme of things, and to know the wickedness of folly and the foolishness that is madness. ²⁶ And I find something more bitter than death: the woman whose heart is snares and nets, and whose hands are fetters. He who pleases God escapes her, but the sinner is taken by her. ²⁷ Behold, this is what I found, says the Preacher, while adding one thing to another to find the scheme of things—²⁸ which my soul has sought repeatedly, but I have not found. One man among a thousand I found, but a woman among all these I have not found. ²⁹ See, this alone I found, that God made man upright, but they have sought out many schemes. (vv. 25–29)

✦ How does Proverbs 7:4–27 shed light on the sort of woman the Preacher describes, one "whose heart is snares and nets, and whose hands are fetters"?

✦ The Preacher isn't being misogynistic here, although it's true that in his culture women were generally considered inferior to men. Rather than focus on any comparison of the sexes, we need to understand what he is saying about the entire human race. What is his conclusion?

✛ The Preacher finds much of life a mystery, but one thing he is sure of: "See, this alone I found, that God made man upright, but they have sought out many schemes" (v. 29). If that were the final word in this perplexing book, we'd feel hopeless were it not for what God has done to rescue us from ourselves. Read Romans 8:28–39 and list some specifics of this great rescue.

....

....

....

....

LET'S TALK

1. Discuss why the topic of death is taboo in our society. Why is it good to remember death rather than avoid facing its reality? If you have been confronted with death in recent months or the prospect of it, how has it shaped or reshaped your relationship with God, your view of the gospel, and the way you share your faith?

....

....

....

....

....

....

....

2. Do you long for the "good old days"? Describe what it is you long for, and why it holds an ongoing appeal. Talk too about why the Preacher counsels against nostalgia, about what underlies it, and about what makes nostalgia different from simple remembrance of times past.

_____

_____

_____

_____

_____

_____

_____

_____

THE BEAUTY OF WISDOM

ECCLESIASTES 8:1-17

Wisdom is front and center in Ecclesiastes, and we're at a good point in our study for a reminder of what wisdom—biblical wisdom—actually *is*. The Preacher seeks it, commends it, and shows us through his observations of the world what wisdom is—and isn't. We can define *wisdom* with words like "insight" and "discernment" and "knowledge," but according to the Bible, those traits are actually the *fruit* of wisdom. A suffering man named Job (his book is another of the Bible's Wisdom Books) provides the truest definition: "Behold, the fear of the Lord, that is wisdom" (Job 28:28). So what does it mean to fear the Lord? It's to hold him in reverent awe. It's to orient our entire lives around him, his ways, and his words. If we live such vertically oriented lives, our horizontal view—how we see this world and everything in it—will be characterized by the fruit of wisdom, which includes insight and discernment. What we focus on shapes how we think, how we feel, and how we live. As someone once said, "We are always conformed to that upon which we center our interest and love." Always. No exceptions. Holding onto this understanding of true, biblical wisdom is the key to profiting from all the Preacher says in this week's lesson.

1. THE FACE OF WISDOM (8:1)

The Preacher begins this section by posing two rhetorical questions, the kind of question designed to get us thinking:

> ¹ Who is like the wise?
>   And who knows the interpretation of a thing?

A man's wisdom makes his face shine,
and the hardness of his face is changed. (v. 1)

The answers to these questions become clearer as we work our way through Ecclesiastes 8.

✦ Why do you think wisdom—the true, biblical kind—changes someone's outward appearance?

....

....

....

....

2. A TIME AND A WAY (8:2-9)

The Preacher has sage advice for how to live wisely under authority, at times unwise authority:

> ² I say: Keep the king's command, because of God's oath to him. ³ Be not hasty to go from his presence. Do not take your stand in an evil cause, for he does whatever he pleases. ⁴ For the word of the king is supreme, and who may say to him, "What are you doing?" ⁵ Whoever keeps a command will know no evil thing, and the wise heart will know the proper time and the just way. ⁶ For there is a time and a way for everything, although man's trouble lies heavy on him. ⁷ For he does not know what is to be, for who can tell him how it will be? ⁸ No man has power to retain the spirit, or power over the day of death. There is no discharge from war, nor will wickedness deliver those who are given to it. ⁹ All this I observed while applying my heart to all that is done under the sun, when man had power over man to his hurt. (vv. 2–9)

In this section, the Preacher is speaking directly to those who serve rulers in some sort of advisory capacity. Even so, the principles he sets out here apply to all of us since we all live under the authority of government officials, bosses, and other types of decision makers.

✦ What does the Preacher guide for wise dealings with unwise leaders?

....

....

✦ We need not fear what rulers might do to us. What limitations do all rulers have, whether wise or wicked?

✦ How do the following passages shape our understanding of how we can live wisely under ungodly authorities?

· Acts 5:29–32

· Romans 13:1–7

· 1 Timothy 2:1–4

3. DECEPTIVE APPEARANCES (8:10–14)

Things aren't always what they seem. We see a bit of this in verses 10–14, but it takes wisdom—the fear of the Lord—to keep this truth in view:

> ¹⁰ Then I saw the wicked buried. They used to go in and out of the holy place and were praised in the city where they had done such things. This also is vanity. ¹¹ Because the sentence against an evil deed is not executed speedily, the heart of the children of man is fully set to do evil. ¹² Though a sinner does evil a hundred times and prolongs his life, yet I know that it will be well with those who fear God, because they fear before him. ¹³ But it will not be well with the wicked, neither will he prolong his days like a shadow, because he does not fear before God.
>
> ¹⁴ There is a vanity that takes place on earth, that there are righteous people to whom it happens according to the deeds of the wicked, and there are wicked people to whom it happens according to the deeds of the righteous. I said that this also is vanity. (vv. 10–14)

✦ What injustice does the Preacher identify in this passage?

....

....

....

....

✦ The Preacher exposes the reality of the human heart in verse 11 as "fully set to do evil." Fueling such evil is the fact that judgment for sin isn't always immediate. Even if it were, however, the human heart is still set on evil. What is necessary for genuine heart change, and how is this pictured in what God says in Ezekiel 36:26–27?

....

....

....

....

✢ The final outcome for the wicked and for regenerate believers has already been determined, even though we cannot yet see it. What is the end for each, according to Jesus's teaching in Matthew 13:36–43?

4. REJOICE AND ENJOY (8:15-17)

Once again the Preacher prescribes how to live contentedly in a presently unjust world:

> ¹⁵ And I commend joy, for man has nothing better under the sun but to eat and drink and be joyful, for this will go with him in his toil through the days of his life that God has given him under the sun. (v. 15)

This is the third time we've been encouraged to enjoy life's simple pleasures as we live our lives in a troubling world. Here, the Preacher commends joy specifically, and while of course we want joy, sometimes, when life's difficulties press in on us, joy seems hard to come by.

✢ To help you understand the Preacher's commendation, fill in the "Joy" chart that follows. The number of passages in the chart provides opportunity for a deep dive, but simply choose just a few if your study time is limited.

Joy	
	Source or Fruit of Joy
Nehemiah 8:10	
Psalm 63:5-8	

Joy	
	Source or Fruit of Joy
Proverbs 10:28, 17:22	
Habakkuk 3:18-19	
John 15:10-11	
John 16:23-24	
Romans 15:13	
Galatians 5:19-24	
Philippians 4:4-7	
1 Thessalonians 5:16-18	
Hebrews 10:32-35	
James 1:2-4	

Enjoying God's gifts blesses us and glorifies God, even when so many of our big-picture questions go unanswered:

> ¹⁶ When I applied my heart to know wisdom, and to see the business that is done on earth, how neither day nor night do one's eyes see sleep, ¹⁷ then I saw all the work of God, that man cannot find out the work that is done under the sun. However much man may toil in seeking, he will not find it out. Even though a wise man claims to know, he cannot find it out. (vv. 16–17)

✦ What does this passage convey about:

· God:

....

....

....

· Human beings:

....

....

....

"If any of you lacks wisdom, let him ask God,
who gives generously to all without reproach,
and it will be given him." (James 1:5)

✦ How does Psalm 131:1–3 help us process the Preachers words in 8:16–17?

....

....

....

....

LET'S TALK

1. The Preacher says that the face of a wise person shines. What do you think this looks like? Describe a wise woman you know. Why and how does wisdom make her attractive? If you have time, consider a time when spiritual growth has noticeably changed you or someone you know.

2. Are you characterized by joy? If not, what hindrances can you identify, and how can you change those hindrances?

LIVE IT UP!

ECCLESIASTES 9:1-18

Through my friend Doug O'Donnell, I learned of an old *Peanuts* cartoon, and a portion of it is too good not to include here:

> Snoopy is atop his doghouse, typing away. Charlie Brown arrives on the scene and is handed what Snoopy has written. It reads, "As it says in the ninth chapter of Ecclesiastes, 'a living dog is better than a dead lion.'" Charlie Brown gives the paper back and asks, "What does *that* mean?" Snoopy examines it and replies, "I don't know, but I agree with it."[21]

This week we're going to examine what the Preacher *did* mean when he wrote those words (9:4). The context is death, a subject we won't fully leave again as we complete our study. The Preacher wants us to look fully at the reality of death and all its implications—not an easy topic to focus on, but as we'll see, it's important that we do. We end on a lighter note, however, as the Preacher gives us a biblical framework for how to enjoy the good things in life and why it's right to enjoy them.

1. IN GOD'S HANDS (9:1-6)

The Preacher has just finished telling us, at the end of chapter 8, that much of what God does remains a mystery. Here we see that the Preacher has accepted his inability to comprehend God's ways, including the inevitability of death:

¹But all this I laid to heart, examining it all, how the righteous and the wise and their deeds are in the hand of God. Whether it is love or hate, man does not know; both are before him. ²It is the same for all, since the same event happens to the righteous and the wicked, to the good and the evil, to the clean and the unclean, to him who sacrifices and him who does not sacrifice. As the good one is, so is the sinner, and he who swears is as he who shuns an oath. ³This is an evil in all that is done under the sun, that the same event happens to all. Also, the hearts of the children of man are full of evil, and madness is in their hearts while they live, and after that they go to the dead. (vv. 1–3)

✦ Living wisely brings blessing, just as folly brings trouble, sooner or later. Even so, there are limits to wisdom's blessings. What does the Preacher reveal those limits to be in verses 1–3?

....

....

....

....

After the coming of Christ, God's people had a fuller picture of life after death. Before Christ, the picture was more veiled, as is evidenced in what the Preacher says next:

⁴But he who is joined with all the living has hope, for a living dog is better than a dead lion. ⁵For the living know that they will die, but the dead know nothing, and they have no more reward, for the memory of them is forgotten. ⁶Their love and their hate and their envy have already perished, and forever they have no more share in all that is done under the sun. (vv. 4–6)

✦ As he ponders death, where does the Preacher place his hope?

....

....

....

....

✛ What do we learn in 1 Corinthians 15:12–26 about death and what happens afterward?

✛ What do we learn from 1 Corinthians 15:42–56 about what will happen when Christ returns on the last day?

✛ With death and the afterlife in mind, what does Paul conclude in 1 Corinthians 15:58, and how does it transform the Preacher's observation in Ecclesiastes 9:5–6?

> *"Death is an enemy (1 Cor. 15:26),*
> *but it is also an evangelist."*[22]

2. EAT, DRINK, AND BE MERRY! (9:7-9)

Given the inevitability of death, the Preacher once again recommends joy, naming some specific situations in which to experience it:

[7] Go, eat your bread with joy, and drink your wine with a merry heart, for God has already approved what you do.

    [8] Let your garments be always white. Let not oil be lacking on your head.

    [9] Enjoy life with the wife whom you love, all the days of your vain life that he has given you under the sun, because that is your portion in life and in your toil at which you toil under the sun. (vv. 7–9)

When we live our lives in the fear of the Lord, orienting everything we do around God, his ways, and his word, we know a freedom that enables us to enjoy God's gifts and the pleasures they bring. At earlier points in the book, the Preacher has guided us toward the simple daily pleasures of eating and drinking. Here he adds the gift of marriage as a source of pleasure and enjoyment. White garments and oil often symbolize joy in the Bible,[23] and whether they accompany a feast or a night of wedded bliss, the idea is to partake with delight.

	Joy in Eating and Drinking
2:24-25	"There is nothing better for a person than that he should eat and drink and find enjoyment in his toil. This also, I saw, is from the hand of God, for apart from him who can eat or who can have enjoyment?"
3:13	"Everyone should eat and drink and take pleasure in all his toil—this is God's gift to man."
5:18	"Behold, what I have seen to be good and fitting is to eat and drink and find enjoyment in all the toil with which one toils under the sun the few days of his life that God has given him, for this is his lot."
8:15	"I commend joy, for man has nothing better under the sun but to eat and drink and be joyful, for this will go with him in his toil through the days of his life that God has given him under the sun."
9:7	"Go, eat your bread with joy, and drink your wine with a merry heart, for God has already approved what you do."

✤ The Preacher has guided us repeatedly to eat and drink with joy, and he will do so again before the book is over. Given the repetition, we should pause and really take notice. Not only is this practical wisdom for daily life, but it also foreshadows a much greater feasting yet to come. And this fuller feast involves a marriage! What do we learn about this wedding feast in Revelation 19:6–9?

3. WITH ALL YOUR MIGHT (9:10)

Broadening out the way to live a full and joy-filled life, the Preacher adds this:

> ¹⁰ Whatever your hand finds to do, do it with your might, for there is no work or thought or knowledge or wisdom in Sheol, to which you are going. (v. 10)

✤ The Preacher's primary point here is about living to the fullest while we can, because a day will come when we no longer can. How does 1 Corinthians 13:8–12 transform what the Preacher writes here in verse 10?

4. A WAKE-UP CALL FOR CONTROL FREAKS (9:11–17)

One of the most challenging aspects of life is how little control any of us has:

> ¹¹ Again I saw that under the sun the race is not to the swift, nor the battle to the strong, nor bread to the wise, nor riches to the intelligent, nor favor to those with knowledge, but time and chance happen to them all. ¹² For man does not know his time. Like fish that are taken in an evil net, and like birds that are

caught in a snare, so the children of man are snared at an evil time, when it suddenly falls upon them. (vv. 11–12)

What the world sees as "time and chance," God's people know as divine providence. When the Preacher uses the expression "time and chance," he isn't denying God's control; he's simply pointing out how things appear to happen.

✦ The Preacher observes that "the race is not to the swift, nor the battle to the strong, nor bread to the wise, nor riches to the intelligent, nor favor to those with knowledge" (v. 11). How do his words speak into your own motivations for the things you are pursuing in your life?

....

....

....

....

✦ What point is the Preacher making with the images of nets and snares in verse 12?

....

....

....

....

The Preacher illustrates his current theme by means of a story:

¹³ I have also seen this example of wisdom under the sun, and it seemed great to me. ¹⁴ There was a little city with few men in it, and a great king came against it and besieged it, building great siegeworks against it. ¹⁵ But there was found in it a poor, wise man, and he by his wisdom delivered the city. Yet no one remembered that poor man. ¹⁶ But I say that wisdom is better than might, though the poor man's wisdom is despised and his words are not heard. (vv. 13–16)

✦ What wisdom is presented here in his story?

....

....

....

....

The Preacher then makes one additional point:

> [17] The words of the wise heard in quiet are better than the shouting of a ruler among fools. [18] Wisdom is better than weapons of war, but one sinner destroys much good. (vv. 17–18)

✦ For all its power, what is one thing human wisdom cannot do?

....

....

....

....

LET'S TALK

1. The Preacher counsels, "Enjoy life with the wife whom you love, all the days of your vain life" (9:9). Notice that he doesn't qualify this love with an *if*—"If you love . . ." Rather, he assumes it as a fact. He can state it this way only when love is a choice, not a feeling. Talk about the wisdom underlying this truth and how it runs counter to the ways people view marital enjoyment today. How can the Preacher's counsel reshape our own viewpoint? Personalize your answer.

....

....

....

_____

_____

_____

_____

_____

2. Ecclesiastes 9:10 isn't the only place in Scripture where we're told to work with all our might. The Preacher advocates working hard because, in essence, we have one short life in which to do so. Discuss how Colossians 3:23–24 shows us a much fuller picture of this concept. Talk about your own approach to work and how both passages, Ecclesiastes 9:10 and Colossians 3:23–24, reshape or influence your motivation.

_____

_____

_____

_____

_____

_____

_____

_____

NO LAUGHING MATTER

ECCLESIASTES 10:1-11:6

We get why wisdom is vitally important, but perhaps we don't view folly or foolishness as equally weighty. We might associate folly with *fun* and *funny*, if we're regularly exposed to expressions like, "She made a fool out of me with that practical joke." The word is also used for tinkering with something, like when we ask, "Hey, did you fool with my phone settings?" There is even a chilled dessert called "fool," made with pureed fruit mixed with whipped cream or custard.[24] So the word *fool* has a variety of meanings in everyday life, but there is only one biblical meaning, and there's nothing funny about it. This week foolishness or folly is linked to the smell of rot and also to serpents (twice!). Folly wears happy, silly disguises, but its true nature is eventually exposed. Ultimately, a fool is someone who rejects the Lord and scorns his word and ways. And the outcome is never, ever funny.

1. A FOOL HERE, A FOOL THERE (10:1-7)

We left off last week noting that "one sinner destroys much good" (9:18). Now the Preacher gives us a potent illustration of this truth:

> 1 Dead flies make the perfumer's ointment give off a stench;
>   so a little folly outweighs wisdom and honor. (10:1)

Likely attracted by the fragrance, these insects alight on the ointment and die, spoiling the ointment as they decay. *Ewww!* The Hebrew words the Preacher used actually mean "flies of death."[25]

✦ What does this imagery convey about the true nature of folly?

....

....

....

....

The Preacher makes a few more contrasts between wisdom and folly:

> 2 A wise man's heart inclines him to the right,
>   but a fool's heart to the left.
> 3 Even when the fool walks on the road, he lacks sense,
>   and he says to everyone that he is a fool.
> 4 If the anger of the ruler rises against you, do not leave your place,
>   for calmness will lay great offenses to rest. (10:2–4)

"Right" and "left" have to do with morals, the right indicating good moral conduct and the left, bad conduct.[26]

✦ What is the Preacher teaching us about folly in 10:3? (If you aren't sure, take a look at Proverbs 13:16.)

....

....

....

....

✦ A ruler's advisors are addressed in 10:4, but the principle can apply to how any of us respond to authority figures. Where in your life would the Preacher's instructions prove wise?

....

....

....

....

In his study of the world, the Preacher has observed another "evil":

> [5] There is an evil that I have seen under the sun, as it were an error proceeding from the ruler: [6] folly is set in many high places, and the rich sit in a low place. [7] I have seen slaves on horses, and princes walking on the ground like slaves. (10:5–7)

🕊 What reality about the world is he highlighting here?

....

....

....

....

2. DANGER ZONE (10:8–11)

The Preacher contrasts more wise and foolish behaviors:

> [8] He who digs a pit will fall into it,
>   and a serpent will bite him who breaks through a wall.
> [9] He who quarries stones is hurt by them,
>   and he who splits logs is endangered by them.
> [10] If the iron is blunt, and one does not sharpen the edge,
>   he must use more strength,
>   but wisdom helps one to succeed.
> [11] If the serpent bites before it is charmed,
>   there is no advantage to the charmer. (10:8–11)

🕊 The actions he describes in these verses aren't sinful, but they can be dangerous. In what way can each of these actions be done wisely or foolishly?

· Working with tools:

....

....

....

· Handling a snake:

Serpents—a creature we find elsewhere in Scripture—are mentioned twice in this passage. How are serpents portrayed in the following passages?

· Genesis 3:1

· 2 Corinthians 11:3

· Revelation 12:7–9

The Preacher's words point us forward to Jesus, who illustrated similar teaching by means of serpents. What point does Jesus make in Matthew 10:16?

3. A WAY WITH WORDS (10:12-15)

The next set of proverbs is primarily about how we use our words—a prominent theme in biblical wisdom, especially in the book of Proverbs. The Preacher writes:

> ¹² The words of a wise man's mouth win him favor,
>   but the lips of a fool consume him.
> ¹³ The beginning of the words of his mouth is foolishness,
>   and the end of his talk is evil madness.
> ¹⁴ A fool multiplies words,
>   though no man knows what is to be,
>   and who can tell him what will be after him? (10:12–14)

✢ How are the wise and the foolish affected by the words they speak?

· The wise:

··

··

··

· The foolish:

··

··

✢ What particular speech folly is exposed in 10:14?

··

··

··

··

Not only the fool's words but also his work proves futile:

¹⁵ The toil of a fool wearies him,
for he does not know the way to the city. (10:15)

The fool works but has no goal in mind, perhaps because he is so busy talking that he hasn't bothered to plan ahead!

4. DISCERNING THE TIME (10:16-20)

God's good gifts can be enjoyed in wisdom or abused in folly:

¹⁶ Woe to you, O land, when your king is a child,
and your princes feast in the morning!
¹⁷ Happy are you, O land, when your king is the son of the nobility,
and your princes feast at the proper time,
for strength, and not for drunkenness!
¹⁸ Through sloth the roof sinks in,
and through indolence the house leaks.
¹⁹ Bread is made for laughter,
and wine gladdens life,
and money answers everything. (10:16–19)

The king's youth in verse 16 has more to do with maturity than with age. And when the Preacher speaks of fit kings as coming from noble lineage, it's because in his day and age, such backgrounds enabled the necessary education and training to lead and rule effectively.

🖑 As you consider the main point he is making, what makes feasting either wise or foolish?

🖑 How do sinking roofs and leaking houses tie into the Preacher's theme in this passage?

> *"The accumulation of references to flies, death, serpents, and the threatening fury of rulers in this section teach the lesson that, if Jesus is the perfect embodiment of wisdom (1 Cor. 1:24, 30), then the Devil must be the true embodiment of folly."*[27]

✦ The resources named in verse 19—bread, wine, and money—can bless or destroy depending on whether they are handled with wisdom or folly. Keeping in mind all you've learned in our study from the Preacher's worldview, fill in the following "Handling God's Gifts" chart as it pertains to the effects these resources can have on us.

Handling God's Gifts

	Enjoyed	Destroyed
Feasting (Bread)		
Drinking Alcohol (Wine)		
Money		

The Preacher adds another important bit of wisdom:

> ²⁰ Even in your thoughts, do not curse the king,
>   nor in your bedroom curse the rich,
> for a bird of the air will carry your voice,
>   or some winged creature tell the matter. (10:20)

✦ Included in a passage that contains much warning about when, what, and how we speak, what wisdom do you think he is passing along to us here?

....

....

....

....

5. FUTURE UNKNOWN (11:1-6)

How we live today will greatly influence our future and that of others:

> ¹ Cast your bread upon the waters,
>   for you will find it after many days.
> ² Give a portion to seven, or even to eight,
>   for you know not what disaster may happen on earth.
> ³ If the clouds are full of rain,
>   they empty themselves on the earth,
> and if a tree falls to the south or to the north,
>   in the place where the tree falls, there it will lie.
> ⁴ He who observes the wind will not sow,
>   and he who regards the clouds will not reap. (11:1–4)

Bible interpreters don't agree on how to best understand 11:1. Casting bread on the waters might have to do with taking a chance on certain business ventures, or it might be about sacrificial giving. This second interpretation aligns well with the next verse. In either case, it seems to be about not hoarding our resources of time, talent, or money—a theme we've seen develop in Ecclesiastes and one that has everything to do with wisdom.

✦ What does 2 Corinthians 9:6–8 show us about why hoarding isn't fitting for God's people?

✦ If we concern ourselves with rain-filled clouds and falling trees, we aren't likely to get much done—a truth clearly stated in 11:4. The Preacher is cautioning us against refusing to choose or go forward in life until conditions are ideal. When can such a refusal demonstrate a lack of faith?

The Preacher describes two mysterious things:

> ⁵ As you do not know the way the spirit comes to the bones in the womb of a woman with child, so you do not know the work of God who makes everything. ⁶ In the morning sow your seed, and at evening withhold not your hand, for you do not know which will prosper, this or that, or whether both alike will be good. (11:5–6)

✦ What two limits to human knowledge are indicated in 11:5–6?

✦ There is wisdom in both acknowledging and accepting our human limitations. As you consider what the Preacher describes in these verses, how can you apply it to:

· Your walk with God:

....

....

....

· Your daily work and the choices you make:

....

....

....

LET'S TALK

1. We're warned in 10:20 that the wise guard their words carefully:

> "Even in your thoughts, do not curse the king,
>   nor in your bedroom curse the rich,
> for a bird of the air will carry your voice,
>   or some winged creature tell the matter."

Discuss where you've seen the truth of this warning play out. Consider not only personal conversations but also social media shares and posts. Where have you experienced the true diabolical nature of folly through careless, angry, or self-seeking words?

....

....

....

....

2. We learned this week that there are times when waiting for—and expecting—ideal conditions hinders fruitful living. Discuss ways to discern when acting is wiser than waiting. Some passages to consider: Proverbs 22:13; Ephesians 5:15–17; and 1 Peter 4:10.

THE POINT OF EVERYTHING

ECCLESIASTES 11:7-12:14

Death is coming. We know that now. But the Preacher hasn't focused on death to drag us down and take our joy away. To the contrary, he has commended joy and counseled us to enjoy all the pleasures God gives. We've seen that, to a significant degree, how we enjoy those pleasures—with wisdom or with folly—determines our destiny. And enjoying with wisdom entails thinking ahead to the reality that our lives will end. We cannot stop the march of time. As they say, our days can be long but our years are short, and the truth of this hits home the longer we live. This week the Preacher points to what's in store for each one of us if we reach those elderly years. Hard as it might be to think about, he explains why it's crucial to ponder. Finally, at the very end of the book, we get to where he's been taking us all along, thoughtfully and carefully through his proverbs and counsel and well-crafted word-pictures, and we discover that life isn't vanity after all.

1. HERE AND NOW (11:7-10)

The Preacher has painted a consistently sober picture of life under the sun, but that doesn't mean we should live a gloomy existence:

> [7] Light is sweet, and it is pleasant for the eyes to see the sun.
> [8] So if a person lives many years, let him rejoice in them all; but let him remember that the days of darkness will be many. All that comes is vanity. (11:7–8)

Seeing the sun here isn't actually about staring up into the sky. His words pertain to our life on earth.

✧ What wisdom is reiterated in 11:7–8 about the wise way to enjoy God's good gifts?

....

....

....

....

✧ The Preacher is making a rather poetic contrast in verses 7–8 between life— "light"—and death—"darkness." He portrays the path from life to death as a trajectory from light to darkness. How does each of the passages below show the reversal of the Preacher's trajectory, how we are taken progressively from darkness to light?

  · Isaiah 9:1–2

....

....

....

  · John 8:12

....

....

....

  · 1 John 1:5–7

....

....

....

· Revelation 21:22–25

"The ultimate remedy to meaninglessness and the
depression caused by a godless life is God."[28]

Until Christ returns at the end of the ages, every one of us will die a physical death. We typically don't dwell on this reality until we begin to age or watch loved ones grow old, but it's wise to keep in mind even when we're young:

> ⁹ Rejoice, O young man, in your youth, and let your heart cheer you in the days of your youth. Walk in the ways of your heart and the sight of your eyes. But know that for all these things God will bring you into judgment.
> ¹⁰ Remove vexation from your heart, and put away pain from your body, for youth and the dawn of life are vanity. (11:9–10)

✦ Given the context, it's safe to say that "youth" here can apply to our productive years and seasons, whatever age we might be. How, according to the Preacher, should we live during those seasons—and do so wisely?

Removing vexation from our heart and pain from our body is easier said than done, right? In fact, it's often impossible. In 11:10 the Preacher is advising us against focusing overly much on personal grievances and bodily pains, because in the eternal scheme of things, these pains are fleeting.

✦ The Preacher reminds us that we are free to enjoy God's good gifts, but the way in which we enjoy them matters (11:9). People who live solely for themselves, with no regard for God, grow increasingly hardened against the ways of wisdom unless the Lord intervenes. Those who have been saved by grace are secure and won't face God's judgment, but we are likely to experience some pain as we learn to enjoy God's gifts rightly. How does Hebrews 12:1–11 show us how this happens?

2. WHAT MATTERS MOST (12:1–8)

Those in their prime—the youth—are still being addressed as we begin the final chapter:

> [1] Remember also your Creator in the days of your youth, before the evil days come and the years draw near of which you will say, "I have no pleasure in them"; [2] before the sun and the light and the moon and the stars are darkened and the clouds return after the rain, [3] in the day when the keepers of the house tremble, and the strong men are bent, and the grinders cease because they are few, and those who look through the windows are dimmed, [4] and the doors on the street are shut—when the sound of the grinding is low, and one rises up at the sound of a bird, and all the daughters of song are brought low—[5] they are afraid also of what is high, and terrors are in the way; the almond tree blossoms, the grasshopper drags itself along, and desire fails, because man is going to his eternal home, and the mourners go about the streets—[6] before the silver cord is snapped, or the golden bowl is broken, or the pitcher is shattered at the fountain, or the wheel broken at the cistern, [7] and the dust returns to the earth as it was, and the spirit returns to God who gave it. [8] Vanity of vanities, says the Preacher; all is vanity. (12:1–8)

What an artistic rendering of old age! The loss of eyesight, bone density, and healthy teeth is depicted here, along with the diminished sex drive and the heightened anxiety that often plague the elderly.

✦ As you consider the Preacher's description of old age, why do you think it is wise to "remember" God in our younger years?

✦ What do you think it means to "remember" our Creator?

✦ Although those of us who live after the first coming of Jesus Christ have a fuller picture of life after death, God's people who lived before Christ certainly believed that death wasn't the end of their story. How is that shown in this passage?

3. THE END OF THE MATTER (12:9-14)

Some Bible scholars think that this final section of Ecclesiastes was written by someone besides the Preacher as a sort of editorial wrap-up because the words are *about* the Preacher rather than *by* him. But there is just as much reason to believe the Preacher authored this conclusion himself. A writer crafting his words in what grammarians call the "third person" (he, his, him) can be used for literary effect. Jesus did this very thing, referring to himself frequently in the Gospels as "the Son of Man." The final section of Ecclesiastes begins this way:

⁹ Besides being wise, the Preacher also taught the people knowledge, weighing and studying and arranging many proverbs with great care. ¹⁰ The Preacher sought to find words of delight, and uprightly he wrote words of truth. (12:9–10)

✛ As you have studied this Bible book, most likely you have formed an impression of the Preacher. What in 12:9–10 either reshapes or refines your view of him?

....

....

....

....

Vital to our understanding of the Bible's Wisdom Books, which includes Ecclesiastes, is the biblical understanding of wisdom. Earlier we defined *wisdom* as the "fear of the Lord," by which we mean a humble, reverent orienting of our lives and our very selves around him. With this definition as an anchor, we can truly grasp what comes next:

¹¹ The words of the wise are like goads, and like nails firmly fixed are the collected sayings; they are given by one Shepherd. ¹² My son, beware of anything beyond these. Of making many books there is no end, and much study is a weariness of the flesh. (12:11–12)

✛ Consider the images used here to describe words of wisdom in 12:11. What effects do such words have upon those who live by them?

....

....

....

....

✛ In each of the passages below, what richer, fuller picture is given for what's described in 12:11?

· 1 Corinthians 1:27–31

· Hebrews 13:20–21

Book lovers might scratch their heads at 12:12, where an endless supply of books to read and learn from is painted in a negative light. But since the Preacher has just finished telling us his love of studying words and arranging them carefully, it's best to see a deeper meaning in verse 12. The point here is that, for all that books are a great blessing, no amount of them can provide us with the knowledge we need most. Only God's words (the Bible) and the living Word (Jesus Christ) can do that.

The final two verses summarize the theme of the entire book:

> ¹³ The end of the matter; all has been heard. Fear God and keep his commandments, for this is the whole duty of man. ¹⁴ For God will bring every deed into judgment, with every secret thing, whether good or evil. (12:13–14)

Viewing the world through the Preacher's eyes has given us a big dose of reality: life under the sun is hard. He has told us repeatedly that "all is vanity"—nothing lasts, and much of what happens seems random or illogical. But here at the end, we see where the Preacher has been taking us all along.

✦ How can we rightly see these final verses as encouraging and hope-filled?

✦ Ecclesiastes 12:14 is the second time in this final section of the book that the Preacher has pointed out the reality of God's judgment. We noted earlier, when we looked at 11:8, that one day there will be a final judgment. What do we learn about that judgment from Revelation 20:11–15?

....

....

....

....

The Preacher declares at the end that "all has been heard" (12:13), but his words are meant to point us forward in history to something more, the full and final end:

> "Where is the one who is wise? Where is the scribe? Where is the debater of this age? Has not God made foolish the wisdom of the world? For since, in the wisdom of God, the world did not know God through wisdom, it pleased God through the folly of what we preach to save those who believe. For Jews demand signs and Greeks seek wisdom, but we preach Christ crucified, a stumbling block to Jews and folly to Gentiles, but to those who are called, both Jews and Greeks, Christ the power of God and the wisdom of God." (1 Corinthians 1:20–24)

LET'S TALK

1. The longer we live, the greater our exposure to the effects of aging as friends and loved ones—and we ourselves—slide closer toward death. It's painful to experience and equally painful to watch. Death is the direct result of sin, of man's fall back in the garden of Eden in Genesis 3. It is a terrible thing, an enemy, but Jesus defeated this enemy through his own death on the cross, where he atoned for the sin of all who put their trust in him. Discuss ways in which observing visible signs of aging can be used as an opportunity to share what Jesus has done to redeem sinners from death.

....

....

....

2. No matter our age, our bodies are decaying a bit every day. Discuss what compels us to strenuously fight the visible signs of aging. Why and how do you engage this battle, and what do you hope to achieve? Talk about how the Preacher's conclusion—the end of the matter—can reshape your perspective.

3. As we come to the end of Ecclesiastes, note what you've learned or what's affected you most about—

· the character of God:

· the gospel of salvation through Jesus Christ:

· the path of discipleship:

HELPFUL RESOURCES FOR STUDYING ECCLESIASTES

Gibson, David. *Living Life Backward: How Ecclesiastes Teaches Us to Live in Light of the End.* Wheaton, IL: Crossway, 2017.

Guthrie, Nancy. "Harry Reeder on Teaching Ecclesiastes." Help Me Teach the Bible. Podcast. May 28, 2020. https://www.thegospelcoalition.org/.

O'Donnell, Douglas Sean. *Ecclesiastes.* Reformed Expository Commentary. Phillipsburg, NJ: P&R, 2014.

Ryken, Philip Graham. *Ecclesiastes: Why Everything Matters.* Preaching the Word, edited by R. Kent Hughes. Wheaton, IL: Crossway, 2014.

NOTES

1. I first encountered this definition years ago from Proverbs scholar Derek Kidner, but it's in common use now.
2. Douglas Sean O'Donnell, *Ecclesiastes*, Reformed Expository Commentary (Phillipsburg, NJ: P&R, 2014), 36.
3. For more detail, see Max F. Rogland, "Introduction to Ecclesiastes," in ESV Study Bible (Wheaton, IL: Crossway, 2008), 1193–96.
4. Justin S. Holcomb, *Ecclesiastes: A 12-Week Study*, Knowing the Bible, ed. J. I. Packer and Dane C. Ortlund (Wheaton, IL: Crossway, 2016), 23.
5. Rogland, "Introduction to Ecclesiastes," 1194.
6. ESV Study Bible, note on Ecclesiastes 1:2.
7. O'Donnell, *Ecclesiastes*, 37.
8. My friend Doug O'Donnell provided helpful insights for this section in his commentary, *Ecclesiastes*.
9. O'Donnell, *Ecclesiastes*, 62.
10. O'Donnell, *Ecclesiastes*, 89.
11. O'Donnell, *Ecclesiastes*, 89.
12. David Gibson, *Living Life Backward: How Ecclesiastes Teaches Us to Live in Light of the End* (Wheaton, IL: Crossway, 2017), 67.
13. Charles Dickens, *A Christmas Carol*, original manuscript ed. (1843; repr., New York: W. W. Norton & Co., 2017), 7.
14. "Our Epidemic of Loneliness and Isolation: The U.S. Surgeon General's Advisory on the Healing Effects of Social Connection and Community," U.S. Department of Health and Human Services, May 3, 2023, https://www.hhs.gov.
15. O'Donnell, *Ecclesiastes*, 103.
16. O'Donnell, *Ecclesiastes*, 127.
17. C. S. Lewis, "The Magician's Book," chap. 10 in *The Voyage of the Dawn Treader*, The Chronicles of Narnia (New York: HarperCollins, 1952), 159.
18. Holcomb, *Ecclesiastes: A 12-Week Study*, 57.

19. Gibson, *Living Life Backward*, 101.
20. O'Donnell, *Ecclesiastes*, 148.
21. Cited in O'Donnell, *Ecclesiastes*, 174.
22. O'Donnell, *Ecclesiastes*, 136.
23. For examples, take a look at Psalm 45 (a wedding psalm) and also at Revelation 7:9–17.
24. Merriam Webster, s.v. "fool," accessed October 2, 2023, https://www.merriam-webster.com.
25. Rogland, "Ecclesiastes," 1098.
26. O'Donnell, *Ecclesiastes*, 184.
27. Max Rogland, "Ecclesiastes," in *Psalms–Song of Solomon*, ESV Expository Commentary (Wheaton, IL: Crossway, 2022), 1100.
28. O'Donnell, *Ecclesiastes*, 221.

Flourish Bible Study Series

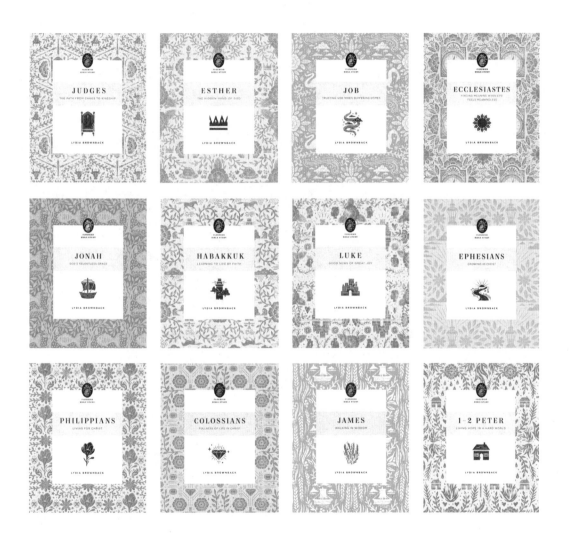